2015
THE BEST MEN'S
STAGE MONOLOGUES

2015
THE BEST MEN'S STAGE MONOLOGUES

Edited by
Lawrence Harbison

SMITH AND KRAUS PUBLISHERS   2015

ISBN: 1-57525-896-X
ISBN: 978-1-57525-896-6
ISSN: 2329-2695

Typesetting and layout by Olivia Monteleone
Cover Design: Borderlands Press

A Smith and Kraus book
177 Lyme Road, Hanover, NH 03755
Editorial 603.643.6431 To Order 1.877.668.8680
www.smithandkraus.com

Printed in the United States of America

Here you will find a rich and varied selection of monologues for men from plays which were produced and/or published in the 2014-2015 theatrical season. Most are for younger
performers (teens through 30s) but there are also some excel-
lent pieces for older actors as well. Some are comic (laughs),
some are dramatic (generally, no laughs). Some are short, some
are long. All represent the best in contemporary playwriting.

Several of the monologues are by playwrights whose work
may be familiar to you, such as Terrence McNally, Don Nigro,
Lee Blessing, Neil LaBute, Sharr White, Carson Kreitzer, Nicky
Silver, Samuel D. Hunter, Adam Rapp, Donald Margulies, Sam
Shepard, David Auburn, Theresa Rebeck and Stephen Belber;
others are by exciting up-and-comers such as Nikkole Salter,
Merridith Allen, Sharyn Rothstein, Emily Schwend, Carla
Ching, Bess Wohl, Zoey Martinson, C.S. Hanson, Halley
Feiffer, Kim Davies and Cori Thomas.

Many of the plays from which these monologues have been
culled have been published and, hence, are readily available
either from the publisher/licensor or from a theatrical book store
such as the Drama Book Shop in New York. A few plays may
not be published for a while, in which case contact the author
or agent to request a copy of the entire text of the play which
contains the monologue which suits your fancy. Information on
publishers/rights holders may be found in the Rights & Permis-
sions section in the back of this anthology.

Break a leg in that audition! Knock 'em dead in class!

Lawrence Harbison
Brooklyn, NY

Seriocomic
Garth Williams, fifties

We are in the 1950s. Garth is an articulate, educated, sardonic illustrator. His new children's book has been criticized in Alabama for promoting racial integration.

GARTH: There's a villain in Alabama, folks, and I have been cast in the role. Yes, I wrote and illustrated "The Rabbits' Wedding." The infamous! The scandalous! The pornographic Garth Williams! A New York City-born, New Jersey-bred, European-educated painter whose subject matter is bunny rabbits. How rare for me to be in the spotlight, as I can usually be found as a supporting player, illustrating books by E.B. White and Laura Ingalls Wilder. Those perverts! It's my parents' fault: My father was a cartoonist, my mother a landscape artist. Everybody in my home was always either painting or drawing. They exposed me to books filled with art from all over the world; the most outrageous and arousing images! And so my goal, like their goal, is to drown children in a watercolor world of the most unspeakable aspects of the human experience. Namely: kindness, tolerance, amity, tenderness, humor, joy, respect for others, interest in the natural world and . . . hope for the future. For the record? Pencils ready? I was completely unaware that animals with white fur were considered blood relations of white human beings. The book was written for children, who will understand it perfectly, as it is only about furry love. It was not written for adults; they are not smart enough to understand its simplicity. It has no hidden political message. It was never intended to wake the sleeping giants of hate. *(Beat)* Anyone with a rudimentary knowledge of art will know that the rabbits are a different color for visual contrast. My book was published in black and white. My inspiration was 11th-century Chinese art. Visual balance; yin and yang; dark and light. As in Chinese scroll art, I just think a black horse next to a white horse looks more picturesque. But that sounds a bit grand, or worse—like an excuse. And I owe no excuses. However, if you're seeking evidence that I am a political rather that pictorial creature, then perhaps you should investigate my other shocking titles: "Baby's First Book." "Baby Animals." "Baby Farm Animals." "The Kitten Who Thought He Was…a Mouse." "Animal Friends." "Home for a Bunny." "Mister Dog." "The Friendly Book." "The Adventures of Benjamin Pink." *(Beat.)* Well, I think we all know what that last one's about, don't we? If you're in Montgomery, Alabama, and you're curious about my latest picture book, "The Rabbits' Wedding," you can find it among 59 other books on the "reserve shelf" of the Alabama Library Service, right where it belongs, alongside the topics of abortion, contraception and communism. My publisher, Harper Brothers, has informed me that my romance about two herbivorous creatures is shaping up to be one of my best-selling titles ever. I couldn't have done it alone. I'd like to thank Senator E.W. Higgins, the great champion of children's literature! We never even knew that we needed him!

Information on this playwright may be found at:
www.smithandkraus.com.
Click on the WRITERS tab.

Dramatic
Ted, forty-three

*Ted has recently been hired along with two others to work at
a sandwich shop in a mall. The boss has disappeared, and
the crew is running out of food with which to make sand-
wiches. Ted has just gotten off the phone with a distributor,
who has refused to make any more shipments to their shop.*

TED: Goddamn it, these people. These goddamn people. The
guy won't even advance me some ham. He was the last of
the pre-approved distributors. Did you know that we are
only allowed to use their pre-approved distributors? But
do you know what else? They're more expensive. They
charge you, the franchisee—forty cents extra per pound.
And it all goes to a kick back to corporate. No wonder
Bob bolted. The poor guy had no chance. 'Cause they sold
him the franchise, it cost, hello—over four hundred and
fifty thousand dollars! But what he didn't know—what
you can't know, unless you read the fine print—is that
they can put your store wherever they want—any crappy,
impossible, dead-end location, they can wait up to two
years to open it. They set all the prices, they control the
supply chain. It's all on their terms! They basically have
you by the balls. They sell you the store; you give them
your balls. How is that fair? What the hell kind of world
do we live in? Where people just . . . People just . . . Take
people's . . . Forget it. I give up. I give up.

Seriocomic
Mr. Much, an imposing man of any age

Mr. Much is speaking to Dr. Kalamazoo, a character who has just realized his life's dream by walking the tightrope before hundreds of admirers. Mr. Much is intent on taking him down a notch, cruelly reminding him of his dull existence outside the Big Top.

MR. MUCH: Welcome to the Big Top. They adore you, doc. That's it. Soak it up. Ignore me. I'm nothing to you now. But what about later? When the lights dim and the Big Top comes down? Where will you turn? Huh, doc? To a memory? To a memory of the here and now? Take my advice and record everything you can about your moment. The smell of taffy. The fantastic lights. The pounding applause. Etch it. Engrave it. Take it all in, because you never know what will stick. You never know which worthless impression will help you through the lonely, loveless nights ahead. Record it, doc. Lock it into the keyless coffers. And tomorrow, when you awake to the white noise of your TV set, I'll be there to help you remember. To help you pretend you can get it back. To carve you a path and show you the way. And you'll follow. Again and again. For the world wasn't created in seven days, as they say. The world, with every yesterday, creates itself anew. And you're asked to make sense of it, to make sense of yourself within it, again and again and again. Sleep well, doc. I'll see you bright and early.

Seriocomic
Ulysses, mid-fifties

Ulysses was once a promising poet but now he's a burn-out, living in a trailer park in the Rockies. His ex-wife, who left him 20 years ago, taking their 5 year-old son, has shown up out of the blue. She has just bought him some groceries.

ULYSSES: This is what I mean about takin' the whole hand. Say hi to you *one* time—bang—we're on a date. Finally admit I'm fond of you—bang—we're in a church. Bad husband to you for ten years?—Bang, you up and leave me.
(Laughs a little. Looks around at the sea of groceries.)
I mean what's the matter, you couldn't fit the entire store in your car?
(Toeing a bag.)
And moon pies? Thought the last box a' moon pies left the factory in nineteen seventy eight—Was probably this very one, these're hairy as a cat. And Fritos, never could stand Fritos—make your whole house smell like socks. You didn't have to do all this, I got a check comin', gonna be here any day; little check, but enough for . . . moon pies. Sammy used to like 'em, though, the Fritos, didn't Sammy like the Fritos? If you'da' let 'im in the mornin' he'd'a' poured milk over 'em. Of course, I like to think that I did let him, though I think perhaps that's a fiction. Why was everything so impossible back then. Some . . . high-wire act seemed we'd never get to the other side of.
(Half amused scoff.)
Guess we didn't. You know, for the first two weeks after you took 'im I actually thought you and Sammy were abducted? Oh, I hollered and carried on, had the FBI come on out to the property, actually tried to punch the sheriff when she said looked like you'd left of your

the sheriff when she said looked like you'd left of your own volition. By then, university already had me on paid leave. Then the paid part of my leave left, too. Along with everything else. In some ways it was a relief, way everything crumbled. I always did find the hardest part of livin' was wonderin' when the other shoe would drop.

Information on this playwright may be found at:
www.smithandkraus.com.
Click on the WRITERS tab.

Seriocomic
"Aunt Susan," twenty-nine

"Aunt Susan" is the pseudonym of a male online advice columnist. He talks to the audience while sitting in a coffee shop.

AUNT SUSAN: Before I became Aunt Susan I worked at Yelp. The internet listings company. I'd sit in a diner like this all day, and shake down the Midwest. I didn't actually work directly for Yelp, I worked for Yelp Premium, a semi-affiliated shadow operation, run by a guy out East we only knew as Steve. We were a kind of hit squad programming—slash—sales force. We'd comb through listings for a sector in a city—Springfield, say, restaurants—and sell upgrades for their Yelp profiles. You might think upgrades, that means it's easier to post? A little extra "customer service," right? Wrong. It's a shakedown. I get the owner, say Ronny from Ronny's Diner, on the phone. I say do you know about our services? He says, nah, I don't need it. But, sir, have you looked at your comment section lately? He looks. He's scandalized. He sees fifteen one-star reviews. He sees a lady saying there was a maggot in her burger. He's horrified. So? Ronny pays for an upgrade, and we . . . "select" the good reviews, the ones that best "suit" his business. What Ronny doesn't know is we're the lady with the maggot in her burger. We're the fifteen one-star reviews. That's what we were doing all week, brutal comment section takedowns of every pet store and shoe shop in Des Moines. You realize, doing this job, the power of words. That word Maggot. I mean, it changes things. It's real. It's not real, but it *is real*. So. Ronny gets rid of the maggot, gets new clean reviews, he thrives, while Manny, next door, takes a dive. Maybe fifty businesses sign up for Yelp Premium—99.99 apiece, we punch out, hit a bar, and next week is the Quad Cities.

Dramatic
Rudolf Bauer, sixty-two

*The great German abstract artist Rudolf Bauer hasn't been
able to paint for 13 years, because he signed a contract
which gives everything he paints to Solomon Guggenheim.
Hilla von Rebay, an artist herself and his former lover, who
negotiated that contract, and from whom he has been estranged, has come to plead with his to start painting again.
Here, he tells her why he can't.*

BAUER: I saw the horror of one war, then the horror of
another one and I painted—I met you and loved you
and painted—I saw priests and whores and mothers and
god—in love in poverty in prison I made form out of
nothing, I saw visions from the top of the earth, from
the cracks in the cosmos because I was free. Then I sign
that? And it was gone. Because when you take freedom
away from an artist? He doesn't just quit, he vanishes.
So I'm telling you that I can't paint. That's the truth.
It's not a matter of spite or grudges. I can't paint, I can't
see, for thirteen goddamn years I can't and it started that
day. Once those lawyers told me what I actually signed
. . . I walked back into this room. And I looked at the
canvas I was working on when I left. That day. I come
home from the lawyers, who said "did you mean to sign
this? To give away your future output?" Output? What
is output? Output is what I'm doing now, not art? But
I pick up a brush like I had for 40 years, I look at the
paint . . . and it curdles in front of me. It turns to mud.
And then I can't see it at all. These pots of color weren't
colors any more, They were holes. Cups of smoke. Can
you imagine? I step back. I back away. I can't see the
color, I can't find the lines, the form, the rhythm I can't,
it's gone. I wait for it to come back. To see something.

For weeks I wait. Months. Nothing comes. Nothing ever comes. I'm blank. Blind. Do you understand?

Dramatic
Ray, mid-twenties

Ray explains to his younger brother, Billy, why it's so important they keep their new job working for the local crime boss, known as Big Bossman.

RAY: Mom was so much better looking than the moms of all my friends, you know. She was pretty, and she was . . . well, it didn't . . . I mean, yeah, sure, my old man was fucking drunk, but who cared, 'cause of Mom . . . *(Beat)* So, that old fuck in there wore her down and by the time she died, she looked like an old hag. Compared to how she looked when we was little, she looked like an old hag. She was twenty years older than how old she really was, in the way she looked. Christ. I never even knew how fucking poor we were until after she died, 'cause she did such a good job of making sure we always had everything we needed. She wanted things for us, Billy. Good things. Better things. And I see the same thing happening to Rose that happened to Mom, I see her getting worn down and haggard and not pretty anymore and looking older than she really is. You remember how pretty Rose used to be? Not as pretty as how she used to be. And a year from now, she'll be less pretty than she is today. I'm not gonna let that happen to her, Billy. *(Beat)* I see the news, Billy, I read the headlines, and yeah, times are tough, but not for everyone, Billy, there are all these people out there, all these no-talent people, getting all those things that Mom wanted for us, not for them, for us, but they're getting those things, not us, they're making money hand over fist, buying all these things, living in these . . . houses, driving these . . . cars, wearing these . . . clothes. I'm talking about morons, geeks, I mean, CEOs, Pop Stars, Porn Stars, Reality TV Stars, Hedge

Fund Fuckers, Wall Street Traders, all these people are so fucking richer than we are, Billy, so fucking unworthy of it, and I'm fucking sick of it. I'm fucking sick of being fucking last on Santa's fucking list, you know what I mean, like a fucking afterthought. I'm sick of waiting, and I'm gonna fucking grab this opportunity while I can, grab it by the fucking balls, I'm going to make something for myself and for this family or I'm going to choke on my own vomit.

Dramatic
Billy, early twenties

*Billy has brought Violet, one the Big Bossman's prostitutes,
home, trying to help her escape to a better life. Knowing
his brother Ray will be angry, he tries to appease him with
a stack of DVDs he's brought home as well.*

BILLY: Aren't you gonna hit me, Ray? C'mon, hit me. It's
o.k. I won't complain. Hit me. I deserve it. Come on.
(Beat) Don't be mad, Ray. Don't be angry. Lookit all the
movies I brought home. I brought home great movies.
Look what I got. I got: "The Alamo," with John Wayne
and Richard Widmark. Only movie John Wayne ever
directed, Ray, did ya' know that? Pretty historical, huh?
Look what else I got. I got: "The French Connection,"
that's one a' your favorites, innit? That's the one with the
big car chase, right? I love that car chase. Best movie
car chase of all time. Without a doubt. Bar none. Except
maybe for the one in "Bullett." With Steve McQueen.
They were outta that one, Ray. But, look what else I got.
I got: "Casablanca." That's a classic, Ray, it really is a
true classic. Bogart's in it. I love Bogart. He's the greatest. Definitely. Bar none. Except maybe Steve McQueen.
Look. I got: "Moby Dick." Greg Peck's in that one. That's
the one about the whale. The big one. The big white
one. The big white whale that eats ships and people and
stuff. Greg Peck's the captain with the big scar through
his face and only one leg. You know the one, Ray. We
saw it on TV when we was kids. You remember. Greg
Peck on toppa that whale, stabbin' it with a harpoon? You
'member? Doncha? Doncha, Ray? Huh? Ray? Doncha?

Dramatic
Big Bossman, anywhere from mid-thirties to around
fifty.

*The Big Bossman, the local crime boss, goes to his employee
Ray's house, and confronts him over his brother, Billy, who is
helping Violet, one of the Bossman's prostitutes, escape to a
better life. After recounting how he punished a former girlfriend, Miranda, for betraying him, the Big Bossman goes
on to explain to Ray their respective places in the world.*

BIG BOSSMAN: People—people like you, Ray—they think,
I will do a job and contract my labor and be paid an
agreed upon amount in return. But this thinking is shit,
Ray. This is a fantasy. You do not own your labor. I own
your labor. And I own the wealth your labor produces. I
own it because that is the way of the world. Great men
own the fruits of the labors of lesser men. You have no
rights to your labor, you have no rights to anything. I
pay you what I feel like paying you. This is why, Ray,
when men like me stuffed the American economy into
the toilet, took a shit on it, and flushed it down the pipe,
the Government ran in to bail us out, make us whole, and
provide us with hand-jobs for good measure. The economy is hemorrhaging three quarters of a million jobs
a month, but men like me are raking it in hand over fist
while men like you cannot put together enough to pay the
rent. You are my bitch, Ray. Every bit as much as Violet
is. Every bit as much as Miranda was. I could make you
dance a jig if I wanted to. I could fuck you in front of
your entire family, were I so inclined. I could tattoo my
brand on your ass, if I so choose. I could suck out your
eyeballs and skull fuck your brains, Ray. Everyone in this
room is my bitch. Even your sister, Rose. I could strip
her naked, too, just like you. I could carve my initials

on her tits. I could fuck her right in front of you. I could make you fuck her right in front of me and your entire family. Right now. I think I will.

Dramatic

Curtis, mid-sixties to early seventies

Curtis, the drunken patriarch of his family, has risen from bed—something he hasn't done in a long time. He finds the Big Bossman, the local crime boss, in his living room, and proceeds to tell him about the reality TV show he was watching.

CURTIS: I fell asleep watching a game show— "Surviving Chains of Love and Death," I think it was called. It involved a series of couples, men and women. Each couple was stripped naked, chained at the ankles, and sent off to fend for themselves on a hostile, jungle island. They were also chased by professional hunters, with high powered rifles. If a hunter caught a couple, they shot the male, and had his head mounted in the hunter's lodge. At the end of every week, the females whose males had been shot were eaten by the other contestants. Also, when two couples met in the jungle, the two men fought to the death. The winner claimed the female. Her chain was attached to his, so then he had two females chained to his ankles. The idea was, the man who had the most women chained to him won the game. But the trick was, the more women a man had chained to his ankles, the easier target he was for the hunters with their high-powered rifles. *(Beat)* There was this one little lady, though. Real spitfire. Her mate was killed by another man, and then she turned the tables and killed that man. Killed his mate, too. Bashed 'em both in the head with a rock. Then she chewed off the foot of her dead mate, and she took to the jungle by herself, trying to avoid the hunters and the other couples. Turned out, at the end, she was the only one left standing. *(Beat)* She didn't win the million bucks, though. She was disqualified. Didn't play by the rules of the game. *(Beat)* Then, I fell asleep and I had a little dream. Stirred me up. *(Beat)* Care to join me for some fortification, Mister?

Seriocomic
Philip, early sixties

Philip's house has been demolished by Hurricane Sandy, as has the house of his friends, the Murphys. Here, he tells them how he almost forgot to rescue his dog. Sal is the Murphy's eldest son, who has come out to Staten Island to help his parents deal with this catastrophe.

PHILIP: It's not easy for us, y'know. There's nothing easy about it. We thought we left Mr. Figgy behind. We'd been in such a rush to leave, shoving things into bags . . . I had the dog case, but no dog. *(to MARTY)*
You know how I feel about that ankle-biting yapper. Always pissing all over everything. *(to SAL)*
When I was a kid I had a black lab, big beautiful dog. Now? I've got a sewer rat in a cardigan. Even so, we're sitting at Joy's, watching the storm come in on the TV, and I felt just as shitty as a man can feel. It was like every news reporter was saying, "Look at this, this violence, this destruction. Nothing can survive this. And *you*, you left your dog here!" *(He shakes his head.)*
Then, maybe an hour into it, Max says "Grandpa, didn't your suitcase used to be by the door?" Now it's halfway across the kitchen, and it's yap yap yap! *(He laughs.)*
We were in such a rush, I must've thrown him in there and forgotten about it. But for that hour . . . And that was just my dog you know? That was just my dog. And I don't even like him. *(beat)* I like to think of myself as a strong man . . . but some things you just can't live through twice.

Information on this playwright may be found at:
www.smithandkraus.com.
Click on the WRITERS tab.

Dramatic
Raheem, African-American, twenty-six

Feb. 1996. Raheem is a failed entrepreneur from the Marcy projects in Brooklyn, NY. Raised in a two-parent home in a working-class family, Raheem struggles to reconcile the sensible expectations of his family and college degree with a sense of self-esteem and manhood he derives from his capacity to access and wield big money. Raheem has orchestrated a sex-tourism trip to Rio de Janeiro, Brazil, for the younger brother of his deceased best friend and another childhood friend to celebrate the first anniversary of the death, and to show off his first successful business venture—a venture he characterizes as "tourism" to them, but is actually a prostitution ring. In this scene, the three men have just arrived in their fabulous Rio hotel suite overlooking the beach, and, Raheem, as the trip's tour guide, gives them the rules of engagement before they venture into the city.

RAHEEM: Naw, son, I'm telling you. I've been here before. You ain't in New York. It look all Gilligan's Island, but there are some rules, some codes of conduct, I got to break down to you, if we're going to have a good time. Rule number one. Don't go nowhere alone. Niggas get jacked all the time when they by theyself. There's just as many Brazilian dudes out there lookin' to come up as there is women. They will jack you. Rule number two. Stay on the strip. Dudes will come talkin' bout, "there are better chicks for better prices further in the city and that if you just go with them,"—uh, uh don't go with them. It's a set up. You'll get there and there will be a bunch of niggas. They'll get you for all your money, your shoes, your jewelry, your passport—which brings me to Rule number three. Don't carry all your cash, leave most of it here, in a safe place. Just in case you get jacked, they won't get you for everything. Don't carry your passport with you neither. The goal is to get here *and* to be able to get back home. It would be different if we lost our passport and we was white, but we ain't. We Black. It ain't no different here. You all exotic 'cause you American, but fuck up and see how quick you just Black again. Rule number four. Arrange the price with these chicks before shit jump off. A lot of 'em don't speak English, but they do speak money. Be real clear. The last thing you want is to be done, tryin' to smoke a cigar and shit, and the chick screamin' you didn't pay her. It ain't worth it. She will go to the police, and they more corrupt than a muthafucka. I do not want to spend my trip in the fuckin' police precinct. I could've stayed in New York for that. Just give her what she ask for and send her on her way. You can always buy another one. And rule number five—don't go home with no bitches listening to no sob stories about how poor they are or how their daddies ain't got no legs or some shit. It's all game. Bitches will be trying to cling to get you, trying to make you feel sorry for them and pay they rent. Fuck 'em and send 'em on they way. Don't get attached.

Information on this playwright may be found at:
www.smithandkraus.com.
Click on the WRITERS tab.

Dramatic
Demetrius, African-American, twenty-six

Feb. 1996. Demetrius is a police officer for the New York Police Department, from Brooklyn, NY. He is married and a father to a five year old daughter, His sense of manhood is largely derived from his ability to be a reliable source of support for his family—a role that gives him an immense amount of self-esteem while simultaneously making him feel like a prisoner to the monotony of life. Demetrius, the younger brother of his deceased best friend and another childhood friend have travelled to Rio de Janeiro, Brazil to celebrate the first anniversary of the death, and to bond via their engagement in sexual tourism: Early in the play Demetrius spends quite a bit of time trying to reconcile his identity as a faithful family man with his deep-seated urge to experience other women. This scene takes place the morning after their first night in Rio as Demetrius and the younger brother prepare for their second day of vacation. The younger brother has just recounted his experience of the previous night—a ménage à trois, alcohol, and lewd parties. Here, Demetrius recounts his experience after being abandoned by his friend Raheem.

DEMETRIUS: Ra was doin' business deals all night. I ended up at this restaurant just to get a drink while I waited for Ra. Take in the scenery. I was sittin' at the bar and this little boy came up to me. Like 9 years old. And he was like, "Mister. I see you alone. I get woman for you." And he pointed to this woman on the beach. And I thought, "Ain't this about a bitch. Brazil even got the children pimpin." So I was like, "I'm good, thank you." And he was like, "you don't like her. You want black one?" And I was like, "No, no. Thank you." And he left with this dumb-founded look on his face like he just didn't understand that I didn't want a woman. So, I was chillin' with my drink, waitin' for Raheem, and like twenty minutes later, the kid comes back and he says, "Mister. You still alone. I got woman for you. You want her." And he pointed to this girl. This little girl. She was like 12 or something. No boobs. No ass. A girl, dog. And I was like—

(Demonstrates his reaction.)

And I thought about my little girl, man. The idea that she—I don't know. So I said, *(emphatically)* "No. No." And the boy starts crying. I realized, them women he was pointing to didn't know him. He just got hip to the game. He was hoping I was interested and I'd give him money. He was hungry. I felt bad, so I took him to dinner. He was just a kid. *(beat)* I told him I was from New York and he was asking me if I know Biggie—like everybody from Brooklyn knows Biggie! I was trying to tell him, but he wasn't trying to hear me. He was telling me his dreams and—this is the crazy part—I looked up from our conversation, I saw that little girl walking with some old white dude off the beach. And I just lost my appetite. For everything.

Dramatic
Demetrius, African-American, twenty-six

Feb. 1996. Demetrius is a police officer for the New York Police Department from Brooklyn, NY. He is married man and father to a five year old daughter whose sense of manhood is largely derived from his ability to be a reliable source of support for his family—a role that gives him an immense amount of self-esteem while simultaneously making him feel like a prisoner to the monotony of life. Demetrius, the younger brother of his deceased best friend and another childhood friend have travelled to Rio de Janeiro, Brazil to celebrate the first anniversary of the death, and to bond via their engagement in sexual tourism. Early in the play, Demetrius spends quite a bit of time trying to reconcile his identity as a faithful family man, with his deep-seated urge to experience other women. Here, he has ushered his two travel companions onto the balcony of their fabulous hotel suite after being caught by them having sex with a prostitute. He attempts to prove to them that his relationship with the prostitute is non-exploitative by telling them what he experienced with her beyond sex earlier that day.

DEMETRIUS: I paid this taxi driver to take us around all day and she took me to her neighborhood—Rocinha, Rochina, something like that. A favela. Like a ghetto. It's right—maybe you can see it from here.
> *(He strains.)*

You can't see it, but it's over there. Behind that Jesus statue. She showed me where Michael Jackson shot that video . . . How's it go?
(trying to recall but getting the words and melody wrong)

They don't give a damn about who we are . . . Remember that? It's crazy crowded, yo. I mean, like even more than New York crowded. Worse than Marcy. It's on this steep hill and the streets are narrow. And the buildings have flat roofs and are built literally on top of each other, but not in one shot. Like over time. It's like, when people want to buy property, they buy somebody's roof and build on top of it. And you look out from the top of the hill, and you see all the mismatched buildings and then you look further and see all the wealth on the coast. It's crazy. She said a lot of people who live in the hoods come from African blood—ex-slaves—and that, back in the day, the masters used to free the slaves for the 3 days of Carnaval to do whatever they wanted. It was a way to keep them pacified, you know, give them something to look forward so they wouldn't revolt. So slaves would wait all year for these 3 days where they could drink, dance, worship, play music, whatever. Dress up. Imitate the rich. Live the dream. And that that's how Carnaval got to be so big in Brazil. Everyone so excited to celebrate 3 days of freedom. Excited to live the dream. Even if it was only for 3 days.

Information on this playwright may be found at:
www.smithandkraus.com.
Click on the WRITERS tab.

Dramatic
Jamie, fourteen

Jamie lives with his mother in an apartment complex near Chalk Farm in West London, the recent scene of rioting and looting, which he describes.

JAMIE: I've got my headphones on and it's on shuffle and it's playing this well slow song. This slow cheesy song that my mum likes but turned up well loud. And I'm standing there, in the middle of the street. Just watching it all. Watching it all play out. And the music is slow and everything looks slow too you know? I know it sounds fucking corny but it's true. It's real. It's like playing out like slow motion, and out the corner of my eye I can see the tube sign like a title caption at the start of a film yeah. Like the start or maybe more like at the end. Just hovering there above everything big bright white letters: Chalk Farm.

And I can see a smashed window.

And I watch kids cycling away from the bike shop on their new wheels.

And I watch more police arriving. Lines and lines of them.

And I'm thinking:

It's not about just wanting a new bike.

It's not about history like what Junior says.

It's not about all anger at politicians or bankers or any of that shit its fuck all to do with any of them cause they're nowhere to be seen. They're not even fucking there.

And it's not about supermarkets on our streets and over-priced fucking ham.

And it's not about saying listen to me. It's not about saying this is what I think.

And it's not about just smashing stuff up for fun.

And it's not about school and it's not about parents and it's not about just grabbing a bottle of something quickly cause it'll make a nice present for your mum.
And it's not about black or white.
And it's not about the police being dickheads.
And it's not about that boy that was shot.
And it's not about revenge.
And it's not a cry for help.
And.
At the same time.
It is. It so massively fucking is.
It's about all that stuff at once. It's about everything.
Everything and nothing.
Right there. A smashed window.
Just everything, and nothing, all at once.

Dramatic
Duffy, early twenties

Duffy is a "cutter" for a boxer. Here, he tells the audience about his job and his world.

DUFFY: I stop blood. Between rounds, so a fighter can keep goin. Call me a cut man. There ain't a better cut man in the whole county than me. And . . . I got me a small garage that my Pop left when he died. It don't make no money, but I ain't complainin'. It's my job. Treats me good enough. Me and my wife, Bug, we live on top the garage. She brings in a little money watchin kids and helpin girls deliver babies. She likes babies, but we can't have none of our . . . I tell her it's like an alky workin' in a bar, but she don't look at it that way. Gotta brother named Fish. Fish is one a them guys just got restless blood in him. Takes on guys twice his size and beats the shit outta them. See, folks got fightin' all wrong . . . technique don't matter, size don't matter. All that matter is who gives less of a shit 'bout what happens to him. Fish win most fights when he looks at em. Guys see in his eyes, he'll die 'fore he'll go down. Jesus. He's a good fighter, but I'm scared now cause he bleeds too much. I try an stop the blood for him. Blood and a weak jaw is what stops most fighters. Once ya start bleedin', it jus keeps bubblin on outta ya. See, fear got your heart beatin so fast and nothin a good cut man can do. Some nights it takes two, three rounds to get it stopped. Two, three rounds not seein' punches comin at ya is a long time. Nine minutes a blindness. Fuck. What ya need is for your boy to take a punch right on the fuckin' cut . . . drive the blood away. But who wants to take a shot on a part of ya that's already hurtin'? I made the mistake a tellin' Fish bout takin' a whack on the cut and now the dumb fuck gives up his eye and dares the other guy ta hit him there. Some guys just ain't right, ya know? Fish got outta jail today. He hit some guy wasn't standin' in no ring and they sent him away. Maybe county settled him down. He thinks I'm borin' cause I don't get shit faced with him down the Lost and Found six nights a week no more. I can sit on the porch and drink beer while Bug reads her nursin' books. If she can get to be a nurse's aid, they make a hunerd bucks a week . . . that extra cash might just help us get by . . . It's a life. I ain't lookin' ta read about myself in the papers or nothin'.

Information on this playwright may be found at:
www.smithandkraus.com.
Click on the WRITERS tab.

Dramatic
Professor Denton, forties to fifties

Denton is a rather windy college philosophy professor. Grange is his prize student. He has been invited over to Grange's dorm room because Grange plans to have a weak-minded fellow student beat Denton up. Grange is upset because Denton never calls on him in class. Denton never calls on him because Grange would then take over his class.

PROFESSOR DENTON: Give you an inch, Grange, and you'll take a mile, I wasn't born yesterday. And I'll not call on you whenever I choose not to call on you.
    (Silence)
Please! Please! This is silly! This is so unnecessary! Let's not argue boys. Not here, not now. There is a Time and a Place. People outside, people everywhere, adding, subtracting, conjugating, sum, est, sunt, two and two makes four, mommy and daddy make three, Jingle Bells, Jingle Bells, God's Reindeer, not Santa's, Santa is a myth, God is real, God is palpable. God brings plague, famine and war. And the Fourth Rider, Death.
    (Turns to them.)
You're young, both of you so young, you put death aside, as you should to get through the day. I see Death in the most unlikely places, in a baby's face, in a bride's demeanor. What should I do, cover my eyes, wear dark glasses? Death is everywhere, people are dying, what do we do, each of us, every one of us, we are all in the process of dying. Isn't this terrible, isn't this horrible, this is a dying planet. We are a Planet of the Dead. Once you understand this concept, once you embrace it, once you accept God's magnificent bounty we can move on to a higher plane. One must acknowledge one's own personal mortality before one can move on. And you, Grange,

your flaw, your fatal flaw is that you can't conceive of the world without you, without your majestic presence, without your grandiose narcissism. You are the center of your own universe. This is what I came to tell you, boys, and now I'm off.

Information on this playwright may be found at:
www.smithandkraus.com.
Click on the WRITERS tab.

COLLISION

Lyle Kessler

Dramatic
Grange, twenty to twenty-one

*Grange is a brilliant student in Professor Denton's philoso-
phy class. Denton has been discussing the existence of God.
Denton never calls on Grange because he would in effect
take over the class; but finally, Denton has called on him.*

GRANGE: May I tell you a story? It is a Once Upon a Time
Story. Once upon a time there was a family who lived on
a pleasant tree-lined street in a pleasant unnamed eastern
city. And in the windows of the house and on the lawn
and on the pavement in front of the house were Down's
Syndrome children, ten, fifteen, maybe twenty of them,
squeezed into every nook and cranny of the house, of
every size and shape, making sounds, some coherent,
some incoherent. The father and mother of these children
continued producing babies in the hope that finally, one
day they would have a normal child. And then one day
their prayers were answered with a beautiful healthy
baby boy. Imagine him sitting at the dinner table with
his brothers and sisters, ooing and aahing, squealing and
squeaking, making noises, sounds, moans, groans, wolf-
ing down their food. I would pass his house every day
on my way to school. He would be shepherding them
around, pushing and pulling at them, making sure they
didn›t wander away or into the street. We would glance
at one another over the years. We never spoke, but we
developed a relationship of sorts. He had the saddest face
I ever did see on a person, a face of terrible misery and
longing. Because this boy knew he would never marry
and beget children! What woman would want to bring
more of the same into the world! And I tell you this story
for a reason, for a purpose. This boy, the normal child,
knows the answer to Professor Denton's question! Go

---

out and find him, wherever he might be and ask him. *'Is there a God?! Is he watching over us?!'* And if he answers in the affirmative, if he says, *'yes, yes, in spite of everything I believe in the existence of God,'* then we have no choice, we too must accept him.

Information on this playwright may be found at:
www.smithandkraus.com.
Click on the WRITERS tab.

Dramatic
Jim, thirties to sixties

Jim Willoughby is an agent of the government and runs a secret program that ensures that Americans remain in a perpetual state of fear. In this scene, Jim is talking to Dave Tamzah, who, in a paranoid fit, has recently blown up his workplace and accidentally killed four co-workers. Jim has just entered the Tamzah home through a secret tunnel in the couch and is urging Dave come back down the hole with him to escape from the police and the media. This means leaving behind Dave's wife, Sonia, who has just revealed that she's pregnant. For Jim, securing Dave Tamzah into the program will help advance the safety of America, as well as his own career.

JIM: If you love freedom for you and your family, you'd better get your ass out of here in a hurry. Look, my job is more than just readiness assessment. I'm like a human cattle prod. My job is to spread alertness, to open the eyes of America a little wider. With a jolt. Sometimes other people can provide that jolt better than I can. People like you. An accident is when you spill your coffee or run over your neighbor's cat. That's not exactly what happened, is it? And now Sonia has a bun in the oven. Is she going to keep it? She's up, she's down, she's all over town. Do you want the spotlight shining on that choice? Every life is precious. At least every American life. Not necessarily equally precious, especially if it's black and poor and in New Orleans. But that's not who died this time. Is it? So now the spotlight is swinging your way, Dave. You and me, we both might get second chances here, see? It's not useful for us to have you and your family destroyed. And this early in a pregnancy . . . Sonia's not a kid anymore—stress and strain pose certain dangers. If you're here, the heat of the spotlight will burn more than just you. Don't fricassee your budding little family, Dave. It's not about me. It's about you. I'm here to offer a way out, an escape route. You're going. One way or another. But this way, you help your family, and you help your country. One way, it looks like you were just another nutcase. A two-day blip on the evening news, and then we're back to crooked cops and politicians sleeping with call girls. But the other way, my way, is productive. People get caught up in the apparent solidity of facts, and they get complacent. And what is complacency? Complacency is three airliners lighting up firestorms of death and suffering over New York City and punching a flaming hole in the side of the Pentagon. Here's an example. Take it as a hypothetical, if you like. Anthrax in the mail. Scary, right? But let's say the bitter old lady sending out deadly envelopes from her home lab gets caught. Everyone goes back to their lives, and forgets all about it, right? But if she can't be found, if there's no trace, then people just aren't sure. It could be anyone. Could be terrorists, or a neighbor, or a scientist. Anyone. When it works like that, people perk up and pay attention. They do as they're told. And that helps everyone. You want to help, don't you? This is a limited time offer, Mr. Tamzah. Oh, they'll love that. "Tamzah." Hungarian? Yeah, see how that plays on the internet. Once "Tamzah" gets out, you might as well paint a big target on your living room window. Or hang a sign—"bricks and molotov cocktails wanted. Insert here." But there are ways to divert attention. The spotlight shines here for just a few minutes, but then we shift it away, over here, over there. But if you stay, they'll hang on to you like a dog with a bone, until they chew you to little bits. Then they'll run off and find the next bone. And what will you have accomplished? Nothing. And there'll be nothing left of you, or her. Nada. Think it over, Dave. But don't take too long.

CRACKLERS
Cassie M. Seinuk

Dramatic
Tom, mid-late thirties

On the second 4th of July after the Boston Marathon Bombings, Tom, an ethnically ambiguous man in his mid to late thirties, has been riding the MBTA Red Line train back and forth for over three hours. When an undercover TSA officer asks him to explain himself and the suspicious parcel tucked under his seat, he must face his guilt and failed attempt at freedom.

TOM: She loved them, like you did, until, like you said, the world changed. Last summer, there we were, walking around the city, just some weeks after the Marathon, you know. And some kids, some kids, set off those firecrackers, probably where Lil got the word cracker from in the first place . . . and there we were walking down Comm Ave, and some idiot kid set one off, I don't know where, but somewhere close enough to sound . . . loud. She worked on Newbury Street, she worked in this small niche wine shop, and she heard the blasts that day, she heard them and for weeks we'd hear a car backfire or a crash down the street, or even just a loud thud from the upstairs neighbors and she'd tense up, kind of like a cat with an arched back, goose bumps. And there we were, right, standing on the corner, ready to cross, and sound of the firecracker, it was so close, and she let go of my hand. It happened so fast, the car horn, the sound, people yelling in the street. In an instant she went from squeezing my hand, to sprinting, to . . . gone. *(beat)* I was going to meet some friends, on the esplanade today. I was getting back out there. I was going to free myself from it all, from thinking that if I had squeezed her hand a little bit harder, held on to her a little longer, she'd still be here. I was going to forgive myself today. I thought I was—I even said I'd bring the Brie. Lil always brought the Brie. But I'm not ready to bring the Brie. We get to bridge, and I tell myself, I'm getting off this time, I'll watch the fireworks, the cracklers, with my friends, but I'm not ready to get off. I'm not. And we go back down into the tunnel and I wait for it to turn around, it goes back towards the bridge, and the cycle continues. I'm sorry if I'm making people nervous, and I'm sorry that I'm causing trouble, but I can't get off the train. Not until they're over.

Comic
Loomer, twenty

Loomer is driving down I-95 with his best friend June. Supposedly, he is delivering the tan Corolla which he is driving to his sister in Florida as a wedding present, but the true reason he signed up for the trip was to track down the new love of his life: a poet named Virgil. He hopes that he and June can bond on this trip, as June has been acting aloof of late.

LOOMER: I don't have any other good pick-up lines, June. I literally became a homosexual like a week ago. So, we're sitting in the living room. Me, him, his grandmother and Aunt Missy. Well I didn't know how to make a move, so I suggested we all play Scrabble. You know I figured we can tire the old folks out. But the Metamucil finally hits his Grandmother, so now she is in the bathroom and Aunt Missy is all upset, because the Grandmother didn't pay for the Metamucil and so she's banging on the door saying, "You owe me this bowel movement! That's my bowel movement!" You know how Aunt Missy is. So I'm apologizing to him, saying, "I'm sorry about Aunt Missy" and then he just . . . He kissed me. He kissed me June. He just laid one on me and kissed me and it was the greatest feeling I had ever had. After everything flushed through his Grandmother, Aunt Missy kind of threw them out. She's a strong lady. And I don't know if it was me being so inexperienced, or his Grandmother's constipation then subsequent diarrhea, but he never called me. And then it was too late for me to call him, or maybe it wasn't, but I didn't. I don't know. But I thought about him—I think about him all the time. All this week, he's been giving poetry readings at random places in Bangor, Maine, like Maude's Bait n' Tackle or the Burger Banquet. I'm so shy, I usually just go and pretend I'm buying some-thing—do you need any shoe laces? But get this—*(He pulls out a piece of paper.)* "Along the Sea: A Poetry Tour along the Coast with Virgil McGillicutty." Bangor, Maine. Myrtle, Massachusettes. Hoboken, New Jersey. Baltimore, Maryland. Shreveport, Louisiana. Napalm Beach, Florida. June, we are going to Virgil's poetry readings. Oh I might not have the courage at first, but I know, eventually, if I keep going to these things, that I'll have enough gumption to walk up to him and say, "Hi, we kissed once while your Grandmother was in my Aunt Missy's bathroom, will you be my date to my sister's wedding?"

Information on this playwright may be found at:
www.smithandkraus.com.
Click on the WRITERS tab.

DEAD SPECIAL CRABS
Dan Kitrosser

Comic
Barney Horntub, fifties to sixties

Aunt Missy has invited Detective Horntub to her Maine house to get him to track down her nephew Loomer, who might get all the credit for a wedding present. Horntub, like most washed up detectives, has a dark past, which he must recount before he accepts the case.

HORNTUB: A hunch is more of something that you feel, than something you know. It could be a stolen set of emerald earrings, a kidnapped pet aardvark gone astray, or even your car keys. If you couldn't find it, with my handy "hunch" I'd make it turn up before the sun turned down. It was a gift I had ever since I was a little boy. My mother didn't need an obstetrician, I found the way out myself. But of course what can be your greatest glory can also be your damnedest defeat. For it was twenty years ago today, Aunt Missy, when I was asked to find something—something so special that I can't even tell you what it was—and all of my hunches they all came up emptier than a swimming pool at an unpopular child's pool party. To make matters worse, I was suddenly framed for stealing the very thing that I was hired to find. I was run outta town, I was, left the force, became a Private-I, and went even more downhill from there. I turned to drink. Not liquor or beer. But have you ever had a lot of soda? Oh it's been a dark time, Aunt Missy, since then I been unable to find the simplest of things. A cat up a tree, a lone sock from the laundry cycle, even the back of my hand. flipping his hand back and forth I mean honestly, which one is the front? The very thing that I was—the only thing that I was—well, I just wasn't that anymore. And the hunches? They simply disappeared . . . until today. I might not fully trust you Aunt Missy, no

I might not trust you at all. But we're gonna find your nephew, Aunt Missy. You and me together. We're gonna find that sonavabitch.

Information on this playwright may be found at:
www.smithandkraus.com.
Click on the WRITERS tab.

Seriocomic
Barney Horntub, fifties to sixties

In pursuit of Aunt Missy's nephew Loomer, Horntub has found him back in his hometown of Myrtle, Massachusetts, a place he hasn't been in twenty years. And on top of that, sparks are flying between him and Aunt Missy.

HORNTUB: Twenty years ago, Aunt Missy, I was on a case. To find two missing children. Oh, all the evidence pointed to the mother. She was a drunk and had a mouth on her to be sure. The husband was dim as a dull light bulb, believed her when she said they were kidnapped, but everything pointed 77 to her. And you'd have to be as dumb as her husband to fall for her. Which I did. Never fall in love with them, Horntub. Never fall in love with them. But what can you do when you're lonely and your interrogating her at her doorstep at night and her hands are trembling as she hands you two tiny little baby hats with her kids' names stitched into them. "Hold onto these for me" she says, "They're gonna put me away for this, so hold onto these hats, they're all I have of my babies." And no sooner does she say this, Aunt Missy, then something magical happened. Now you could say it was a low hanging harvest moon, but I swear to you Aunt Missy, suddenly that dark street lit up with the light of a thousand suns. And this woman, this wasn't a suspect anymore, this was a mother who had lost her babies. And she looks me in the eye and she kisses me. She kissed me Aunt Missy and I fell. I fell harder than math test. Well the very next night there a knock at my door. It was the commissioner. They had a search warrant for me. And in my room, under my bed, there were the hats, just where I had placed them. How could I explain that I had fallen for the suspect? The only other explanation, Aunt Missy, was that I was the one. I was the one who . . . I was the one who killed Abraham and Zelda. I fled. Ran away to Maine where they barely have telephones. No one could track me down. And I vowed never to fall in love with a client again. Yet here I am. In Myrtle Mass, twenty years later, with you, Aunt Missy. *(He turns to her.)* With you.

Information on this playwright may be found at:
www.smithandkraus.com.
Click on the WRITERS tab.

Comic
Jack, fifty

Jack, a TV producer, is on the phone with his lawyer, regarding his pending divorce, while his publicist, Stanley, waits for him to finish.

JACK: *(into headset)* Sweet bearded Jesus, Bebe, what the fuck does that hateful cunt want? Listen, nobody regrets not signing a pre-nup more than me, okay? Grinding my teeth down to nubs and my asshole's drippin' black blood, so spare me the "woulda, coulda, shoulda."
(to STANLEY)
Boat full of holes, tellin' me how wet the water is.
(into headset)
Look, she can justify her thievery until the end of fuckin' time, but it's my money we're joustin' over. Where was she when I was stuck in a writer's room, sweatin' over a second draft and eatin' cold ahi out of a Styrofoam container? Tell you where she was. Sashaying her gooey white ass around Barney's, buyin' shit she don't need and posin' for a camera that wasn't fuckin' there! *(Beat)* Fuck California law and fuck her, Bebe! That maniacal bush-pig wanted for nothin' in our marriage, now she's climbing up my ass lookin' for caramel corn. Fuckin' pirate! Maybe if she'd spent less time doin' bong hits and buying tennis bracelets and more time being an actual, functioning wife, I wouldn't have been cruisin' to K-town every night for kimchi and "suckee-fuckee." *(Beat)* Bring up pre-nup one more time, Bebe, and I will back over your kids with my car. No, you fuckin' calm down! Get that hot-flashin' skank to settle on a number and get it fuckin' done! Now! Now! Now! Now! Okay?

Great. My love to Tovah.
(Hangs up the phone, sighs, then points to STANLEY)
Continue.

Information on this playwright may be found at:
www.smithandkraus.com.
Click on the WRITERS tab.

Seriocomic
Jack, fifty

Jack, a TV producer. is discussing with his publicist what they are going to do about an actor on his show with a drug problem.

JACK: We're the number one scripted program on network television, about to sell into syndication for two million per episode, shutting down is not an option. Stanley, I have been in this business, man and boy, for over twenty-five years, and one of the few undeniable facts I've learned is that if it ain't on the screen, it never fucking happened. Point is! Point is . . . all the little dramas that go on behind the scenes, while annoying and time consuming, if they're not part of the final product and the folks at home can't see it on their television sets, then it's not a reality, a topic for discussion and nobody fucking cares. A First AD takes a shit in a prop toilet. A stand-in goes berserk with a cross-bow, starts picking people off like antelopes. A writer tries to fuck the kid actor's mom. The kid actor's mom fucks the craft service guy. The fat actress won't memorize her lines. Studio heads finger-bang little girls, the earth shakes beneath us and Jesus died on a cross. *(Pause)* And we still gotta put on a TV show. Every week, thirteen-point-five-million people tune into this show . . . my show, to laugh at my jokes. And nobody is going to keep me from my appointed rounds. Certainly not some open-sore little Malibu hop-head who can't keep his nose out of the "yayo" or his cock out of the "cha-cha."

Information on this playwright may be found at:
www.smithandkraus.com.
Click on the WRITERS tab.

Seriocomic
Clinton, thirty

*Clinton has lost his hand in the war and has been kick-
ing around a few years. His aunt knows a hotshot TV
producer and has arranged a meeting for Clinton with
him, during which they discuss a series idea.*

CLINTON: Goddammit, make the setting sweet and romantic. When he finally does fuck her! Make it nice.
Okay? Okay? Maybe a cabin in the woods somewhere's,
candles and wine. And he's real gentle with her and she's
extra tender to him, not callin' him a "loser faggot."
They're kind to one another.
> *(Beat)*

And, and, and when they're done, they share a meat-
lovers' pizza in bed, uh-huh, talk about the future. Agree
on two kids, boy and a girl, Roxanne and Chuck. And
she's gonna be a stay-at-home-mom, while he provides
for the family by fixin' engines and racin' stock cars on
the weekend. That's good, right? And look-ee, don't
worry about runnin' out of ideas, ever! I got enough bad
shit, show could run for twenty years. Dad left before I
was born. Drug-addict mom. In and out of jail. Oh . . .
one time, she left me at her dealers house, as collateral,
while she went to get money at an ATM. You could turn
that into something funny. She loses me at the grocery
store maybe, something like that. Oh, and there's plenty
of supporting characters, 'cause when she went to jail,
I got tossed all over the place, relative to relative, each
one fuckin' crazier than the last. This one aunt used to
toss hot water on me when she was mad. Scalding hot
water. Have to change that for the show. Probably. She
could hit me with a pie! Funny. Put curlers in her hair.

Old bat. Hilarious.

(Pause)

What about that? Think you can make all that funny?

Information on this playwright may be found at:
www.smithandkraus.com.
Click on the WRITERS tab.

Dramatic

Francis, twenties

Francis is a grifter in a family of grifters. He has tracked down his brother, H, who he believes has absconded with an extremely valuable comic book which he was supposed to turn over to their sister, Blue, and an enforcer named Jimmy has threatened kill her. He has just found out that, in fact, H gave the comic to their mother, Mable, who taught them all everything they know about con artistry, to give back to Blue—which of course she didn't do.

FRANCIS: Blue has turned me on to game theory. There's this principle called Brinkmanship. Heard of it? They're using it now in Israel and Palestine. The president was using it with all that fiscal cliff business with Congress. To get someone to cooperate, to stick to an agreement, you escalate threats to big fucking casualties until the other guy has to back down. For instance, with you. If you don't help me find Mable, I will give you to Jimmy. That's right. I am showing you my cards to save us all a lot of time. I need you to think like me. Understand how serious I am. And that if you get hurt, it will be your fault. With other people, I could use other methods. They call them "contract enforcing strategies." I could threaten to destroy your reputation. But you already took care of that yourself. I could threaten to take all your money and bankrupt you. But, I checked your bank account, and I scanned the Caymans and it looks like you're dead fucking broke and there's nothing left to take. So, I want to show you that you have given me no other option. Don't make me hurt you, H. Don't make me resort to violence.

Information on this playwright may be found at:
www.smithandkraus.com.
Click on the WRITERS tab.

Dramatic
Bob Moses, African-American, twenty-nine

*Inspired by actual events, Freedom High takes place in
June, 1964, when black Civil Rights workers trained hundreds of mostly white volunteers to work in Mississippi
registering blacks to vote. This soliloquy takes place just
after Bob Moses, the organizer of the Mississippi Summer
Project, has learned of the disappearance —and probable
murder —of three Civil Rights workers who'd been at the
training the previous week. He struggles with his responsibility for the young people who are about to go into a
terribly dangerous place.*

MOSES: I was responsible. The shooting of Jimmy Travis. The
beating of Herbert Lee. The face of Louis Allen, scattered on
the driveway. Tears and blood, swallowed by the hot clay.
"Speak up, testify, for only if we stand up can we make a
change." He stood up—and was pushed down into the earth.
Young men, moved by my words, became blind to their
safety. Children. Little more than children. Looking at me
like I have all the answers. I tell them, no one can give you
the answers. When you are cornered by a beast, and next
to you are children, no one can tell you what to do. But I
sent them down to Neshoba. I pushed and nearly insisted,
"Bring down a thousand white students. We need our white
brothers and sisters working alongside of us" Attracting the
eyes and ears of a nation blind and deaf to the murder of
Herbert Lee. And now these kids, looking up to me. Don't
look up to me! I do what I must do, and so must you. If you
only do what someone else intends, your death will make
your life meaningless. How do I tell them this? How can I
make them see, before they're pulled over by Mississippi
law? On a dark country road. And must face, all alone, the
long . . . endless . . . night?

Dramatic

Ray, white, thirty-six

Inspired by the Mississippi Summer Project, Freedom High takes place in June, 1964, when black Civil Rights activists trained hundreds of mostly white volunteers to work in Mississippi registering blacks to vote. In this monologue, Ray, a minister working with the Project, speaks to a room full of young volunteers attending a class on non-violent tactics. He tells this story to demonstrate the strategic value of "loving one's enemy," even in the face of violence.

RAY: Let me try to break this down for you all. I was on a march in Smithtown, a floundering little burg 40 miles south of Raleigh. About 30 of us were there, protesting the refusal of the town to register Negroes. This young man, typical small-town redneck, leather jacket, slicked down hair, comes up to me, his eyes are clouded over with rage. He doesn't see me, he's probably really mad about his Daddy, who drinks too much and keeps him down. So this boy with a hint of stubble on his chin pushes me down onto the dusty asphalt, spits on me, and barks, "Get out of my town, nigger-lover." My first impulse—still —I wanna knock that sonofabitch down and show him what for. I still could, you know. But that's where love comes in. I look that boy in the eyes as I pick myself up and wipe his spit off my face. And that's when I think of Pete Robillard, my next door neighbor from when I was growin' up—when Pete was five, he was like a little angel, with the sweetest disposition you can imagine. And I can see, in the face of this Smithtown greaser, the cherubic cheeks and funny chin of 5-year-old Pete Robillard, and suddenly I'm smiling at this poor boy, almost huggin' him, 'cause he doesn't really know what he's doing. I say, "Which fountain here makes the best

strawberry soda? Is it that one, or Rexall?" "'Wha?'"
"You like strawberry or chocolate?" "Uh, strawberry."
Now his friends are starin' at him, but he feels that I love
somethin' in him that his grownup pals never knew. "So
who makes the best one?" I ask. "Rexall," he says. Then
he looks at me real hard. I say, "Thanks." "For what?"
"I'm thirsty. Come have a soda with me."

Dramatic
Henry, African-American, twenty-six

Inspired by the Mississippi Summer Project, Freedom High takes place in June, 1964, when black Civil Rights activists trained hundreds of mostly white volunteers to work in Mississippi registering blacks to vote. In this monologue, Henry, a Civil Rights activist, speaks to Jessica, an idealistic young white volunteer with whom he's become romantically involved. Desperate to make her understand how dangerous the Project is, he shares a secret from his past.

HENRY: I never did realize how bad a place Mississippi is 'till I got to be a teenager, and wanted to go swimmin'. Couldn't use the town pool. For some reason, my brother and I would end up standing outside that pool, watching the white kids laughin' and splashin' and playin'. We kept goin' down there, I don't know why. We'd just stand there. Couldn't look at each other . . . Then we'd go off into the woods and try to kill us some squirrels. One particular hot summer day we couldn't find any, 'cept for this mangy man squirrel that couldn't hardly run up a tree. We'd just come from watching the kids swim, and without a word we put that old squirrel down with a couple big rocks. Before it died, he gave out this cry sounded like an old man. Then we threw some more rocks at it, and just left it there in the dust. I could kill a man like that. You don't know what it's like. They do anything, anything and just walk away, smilin'. I can't . . . I can't let 'em get away with it. You don't understand. . . . See . . . before they got to my brother, they had me. I was canvassing some farmers outside town, and took a shortcut through the woods. Suddenly I was surrounded by the . . . reddest of red necks I ever seen. They were pink with anger, 'cause they heard some Freedom Niggers were talkin' to their colored folk. Five of 'em, with bicycle chains and a big pipe. One of 'em had this big wad of pink bubble gum he kept poppin'. *(pause)* So you know what I did? Jessica? I pretended like I was somebody's cousin, like I was just some sharecropper, payin' a visit from the next county. Started sayin' all this bull jive like . . . "No, suh, I, I, I don't want to get involved in no politics. My family's a good family, we works for Mr. Reed over in Florence, Mr. Reed good to us, we never want no trouble, no suh!" I'm bowin' and movin' my head around like a wooden puppet, and cryin' . . . *(pause)* I'd been beaten before, shot at, jailed in the night. But somethin' happened that day . . . Suddenly, didn't wanna die, not like that. They bought my story, and let me go, with just a kick to my pants. But later, those crackers find out who I really am, and come after me. They come to Mabley, and grab my brother off the street. Friend of the family saw it. "We know who you are, nigger. You takin' a ride with us."

Dramatic
Grant, thirty-two

Grant, who is planning to marry his boyfriend Gary, has told his longtime friend Carrie that he is sick.

GRANT: When I came to at the hospital, that's when they told me something was off. Nobody knew what right then. Took a couple of years and a few more doctors to really nail the thing down, but it started with an irregular heartbeat that was only detected because of what happened. Ironic, really. I never would have known. Not until things got worse. I could say, maybe the big cheese—or divine what have you—works in fucking mysterious ways, couldn't I? I could say that. But I won't. Because what kind of higher anything would . . . It's MS. There. I said it. I've been on some very good medication and some not so good medication over the years. But I'm still me, I'm still moving and so I'm still living unless or until I can't. Sometimes I'm awake at night thinking things like, 90 days until the wedding times 2 pills a day is 180 pills—10 is the number of side effects I'm watching out for—any of which would mean postponing the ceremony until I recover. $100 per plate for the caterers. 365 is the number of days in a year except 366 every fourth year, every one of which I get out of bed hoping not to have chest pains and if I do it's a frantic phone call and a new medication. That's 2 more pills and ten numbers dialed on my phone. 2 is the number of times I vacuum per day. It takes precisely 1.5 hours to do the floors, surfaces and windows in the house. 350 is the perfect temperature to cook a *coq au vin* in the oven. There are roughly 700 muscles in the human body, 23 of which are used to smile. Sometimes I am actually awake at 3am wondering how many more perfect coq au vins I'll cook, or worse, how many times I'm going to smile before any of those muscles will not allow me to do so anymore. 2 is the number of babies I've always wanted. 33 is the number of sexual partners I've had. Scratch that. 34. How many numbers, how many people, how many passion-filled nights will I get before I can't perform anymore, before I can't urinate or breathe or sit or stand up by myself? How many numbers until my husband won't get what he needs from me. How many numbers before time runs out? Numbers, numbers, mother-fucking numbers. Polyamory. The wedding. This house. This chance . . . it's all about devouring life, not wasting a second of time defining our lives by anyone else's standards. And I've learned every important lesson about love the hard way, so believe me when I tell you that THIS IS WHAT I WANT.

Information on this playwright may be found at:
www.smithandkraus.com.
Click on the WRITERS tab.

Dramatic
Yad, fifties

In a war-torn country, Yad tries to get away from it all by smoking tobacco, eating pistachios and drinking arak. But on this particular day, bombs are falling closer—making them harder to ignore—and he is flat out of arak.

YAD: Will night ever fucking fall? I have too many exiles, too many deserts in my throat to cry out. For once I want night to fall close to me, not on the ground but through my fingers. Night always falls all at once. I want it to fall little by little. I want it to fall bit by bit. I want it to fall drop by drop. I want it to fall step by step, into my eyes. I want to tear up the night that's falling on me. I want to spew out the night that's slipping into me. When night falls, I feel it here. When night falls, I feel it bubble everywhere. It's bubbling now, very loudly, in my head. Night bursts forth like a torrent in my stomach. I don't smoke anymore, my lungs are empty. Night steals my breath, it devours my lungs. Night vomits night into my guts. When night falls, it rises up in my throat. I rip out my throat and slice it in two. I slice it vertically from larynx to pharynx. I find a mass grave. A grave where all the nights are decomposing. All the nights that have fallen into my body. I am the mass grave for all the nights that don't know where the fuck to go. When night falls, I plow the sea. It doesn't budge, the sea will never budge. Too much salt, too many books, too many corpses in its depths. I hear jackals lap up the waves. Only jackals have the right to lap up the sea. I hear them, the jackals, vomit stones and black mud all over the beach. The jackals vomit heads of children burst open by explosive bullets. Night falls yet there is white light everywhere. All the stars howling up there and all the tracer bullets shouting in my head. I went into the night once and I came out burned by salt and corpses. Everything is poisoned, rotten, in the night, the sand, the water. The alphabet too is poisonous. The desert too, especially the desert. We're going to eat up the desert until the last grain of sand. We're going to eat up the desert until the last star. Everything falls here: The desert falls. The sea falls. Oblivion falls. Exile falls. The body falls. The tongue falls. Eyes fall. God falls. Night doesn't fall alone.

Information on this playwright may be found at
www.smithandkraus.com.
Click on the WRITERS tab.

Dramatic
Amin, early twenties, a university student

Right after a bomb destroyed the house next door, killing the entire family, Amin finds his father pouring himself a drink, seemingly oblivious to the tragedy.

AMIN: Elias's entire family is gone. The entire family, the father Elias, the mother Mary, the children Jeremy, Nathan, Paul, Rachel, and Naomi. I was there when the accident happened. Little Jeremy was on the horse riding at full gallop. He was going fast, too fast, like a hurricane. He didn't see the roadblock around the corner, a soldier saw the horse coming, he fired a first shot in the air, little Jeremy tried to stop the horse, the horse refused to obey, the soldier fired a second shot, the bullet carved through the horse's neck. The horse reared up, its front hooves in the air, then fell forward in one motion. It smashed the soldier's rib cage. You don't give a shit, I know, look at my hands, you see the state of my hands, you see what I have in my hands, or not, I searched with everyone, after the bombing, I searched, I found this tuft of hair, you recognize this hair, no, you don't, this, this is little Naomi's hair, it's all that's left, I searched, I saw so much flesh mixed in the plaster, I searched, I saw so much blood mixed in the cement, I searched, I saw fingers, I saw arms, I saw feet, I saw skin, I saw eyes, I saw guts, I saw genitals, I saw cigarette butts, I saw rings, I saw fear. I searched, I found the smell of death, do you know the smell of death, it was hot, the smell was rising, it was rising from everywhere, Dad, I thought it was coming from me, that I was the one who stank that much, I tore off my clothes but the smell was still there, stronger than the ruins, stronger than the corpses, stronger than us the living, stronger than all the dead. Then I understood that you lied when you said God is a joke, I understood that you've been lying from the beginning, that if the smell of death is so strong, it's because God is here. Only God can erase the smell of death.

Information on this playwright may be found at:
www.smithandkraus.com.
Click on the WRITERS tab.

Seriocomic
David, early seventies (but could be any age for
audition or class use)

*David, a playwright, is talking to his daughter Ella, an
up-and-coming actress. He is ranting about critics.*

DAVID: See that's what I'm talking about—they're all fucking idiots. They are a sick cadre of pathetic, sniveling,
tiny men with micropenises and no imaginations who
write out of their asses and who love to tear you down
because in truth they know that you are doing exactly
what they could never do—that you are doing the only
thing they have ever wanted to do—and they are fucking jealous. You know that, don't you? How jealous
they are? They're boiling with envy. They want a piece
of you. They want in. They wanna get inside you!
They wanna climb right in! I'm serious. They wanna
fuck you. They wanna fuck you so hard, they're blind
with fuck-rage. And even though they're almost exclu-
sively queers—you think that matters? It doesn't matter! Because the kind of fucking they wanna do to you
is gender-blind, soul-blind—they're blind to it themselves! I mean it's like a fucking snot-nosed kid dipping
your braid in his inkwell! They get a kind of pleasure out
of being perverse. I'm not kidding. Why are you laughing? It's like a pedophile and his prey! Humbert Humbert
and Lolita! She obsesses him and this disgusts him so he
abuses her and then he fucks her, and then abuses her and
then fucks her again! I mean don't you notice how it's
always the brilliant performances that are the ones that go
unnoticed—or even worse!—the ones that get the kind of
condescending, bullshit mentions like: "The serviceable Ella
Berryhill." "The capable . . ." "The reliable . . ." "The sturdy
. . . !" As if you're a fucking stool they enjoyed sitting

on for the evening. Or even worse: just the name, in parentheses—"When Medvedenko confesses to his wife Masha"—and then in parentheses: "(Ella Berryhill),"—Oh God, and then! What's even worse! Just to rub some salt in the wound—just really grind it in—after giving you the requisite, dismissive nod—"Ella Berryhill", (close paren)—then, a paragraph later they'll say: "Well, the real pleasure of the evening is the exquisite performance of—" And then they pick the one person in the cast who's a fucking hack! The one actor who's chewing the scenery as if he just got fucking dentures and he's getting executed next Tuesday! Or the "ingenue"— the girl who's sexy, or (maybe more accurately), what a gay man thinks he's supposed to think is sexy—like your fucking Clementine in your play! Your perfect little "Nina" . . . but that's exactly what they want! A wide-eyed, little brain-dead . . . trout-mouth who clearly only a man terrified of his own mortality would want to fuck!

Information on this playwright may be found at:
www.smithandkraus.com.
Click on the WRITERS tab.

Lawrence Harbison

Dramatic
Pete, Twenty-six

A photo that Pete took of his estranged friend Talya was recently used in a billboard ad that caused a great deal of controversy. Both the photo shoot and controversy have caused Pete to delve back into feelings not just about Talya, but his own self-perceived inadequacies. He is confessing to the audience, but also defending the part he has unintentionally played in the controversy. The billboard is visible.

PETE: I'm not sayin' I've been in love with her all this time. I watched her date a rotation of assholes, and I got kind of disgusted. I mean, I don't know, you do things, you make up reasons not to respect people. So you won't care. I mean, people do that, right? No one wants to be hung up on a girl who's never gonna date them. So, you know, I got over it. Dated other people, smoked a lot of dope, flunked out of school. I mean, not because of Talya. Because I'm unmotivated or whatever. Anyhow, it was the summer after I would of graduated. No . . . two. And all my friends are, you know, launching themselves. Starting their careers. And I got nothin'. Nothing but some pissed off parents and a vague interest in photography. My grandfather had died a few months back, and he left me all his photography equipment. And I thought . . . maybe this is the universe telling me something. I started to put together a book. A website. And I knew Talya had modeled. And yeah, ok, I wanted to see her. So I looked her up, asked if she'd be willing to do a shoot with me. And she said yes. These days I do a fair bit of fashion photography; I've become somewhat desensitized to being around beautiful women in various states of undress. But back then . . . Just asking her if she wouldn't, maybe, mind posing in a swimsuit . . . She was totally fine with it. And yeah, that day, taking pictures, it stirred up some things, old feelings and that . . .yeah. And honestly, when I first felt it . . . I was thinking, no man, just push it aside. Don't go there. We were reminiscing about college, how we first met, and I'm thinking. . .maybe it doesn't matter anymore. That whole out-of-my-league thing. Maybe I'm not. . . I mean look at her, she's laughing at my jokes, we were really relaxed . . . But no, total brush off. Still out of my league.

Information on this playwright may be found at:
www.smithandkraus.com.
Click on the WRITERS tab.

Dramatic
Inventor, forties

"The Balcony Scene": The Inventor, in a university Rotunda, gazes up at his research assistant, who leans on a balcony, above.

INVENTOR: My goodness. She really is something. Such . . . vigor. Such a . . . glow of health. Such . . . cha cha cha. I must speak to her, I must let her know that she has. . . aroused such interest in me. No, I . . . shouldn't. Improper. Don't want to lose this position like the last one. Don't want to disappoint Hannah . A university position is not . . . to be sneezed at. A university position is of value. Something to be maintained. Not thrown away for the sight of a beautiful girl, leaning on a balcony. A beautiful girl who ably assists your research should be valued for her assistance, her quiet competence. Her quick mind, nimble fingers, not her . . . eyes. Of the most piercing blue. So that you must look down. Must look away. Even asking a simple question, "Could you tidy up the titrating burettes?" suddenly is cause for alarm, a hot flush creeping up the neck and you must look down. At your wing tip oxfords. Mute as always in a crisis. Then find yourself, an hour later, here. In these marble, hallowed halls. Staring up at her. Staring . . . off into the distance. What's she looking at? What is she thinking?

Dramatic
Guy, twenties to thirties

The Guy, behind the counter of his comic book store. He's thinking about the Girl he met that afternoon, who came in looking for All Star Comics #8, the first appearance of Wonder Woman in print. He draws. We see what he draws.

GUY: Of all the pulp joints in all the world, she hadda walk into mine. What am I thinking? She couldn't... does she like me? Can I trust her? *(It is coming into shape: the Girl, as a superheroine)*
Or is she lying. Does she just want something from me.
(or...evil vixen?)
Of course. She's just . . . smoothing the way. Using her powers for manipulation. Man-ipulation. I'm being ipulated!
Shit, I'd do it. If I had a body like that.
(continuing to draw . . . she becomes more buxom, more sexualized.)
I'd get my way. I'd get out of speeding tickets (not that I speed, but— *'cause I know I couldn't get out of the ticket.)*
If I had a body like that, I'd speed! I'd tear up the road! I'd get let into clubs . . . part the velvet rope . . . If I had a body like that. I'd be able to do . . . anything.
(beat)
Who can resist that kind of power? I couldn't. I can't. No, I can. She's not getting that book! First outlandish expense of my 20's. Led me to this. Let me know I could do this. Spend my life surrounded by ink and muscle. Story and possibility. Dim, protective lighting and the soft thwip-thwip-thwip of the fanboys rustling through the stacks. I didn't have to go live in cubicle-land, take orders from somebody else, join the evil empire of commercial gack and crap. I could be . . . an entrepreneur. Shit, I'm

an employer! (just two dudes, splitting part-time, but . . .)
I'm The Man. Never thought I was heading there . . . Maybe
I'll give it to her. Sell it to her.
My first. Big. Score.

(He considers.)

No.

(He erases through the drawing. Lines of blank criss-
cross her body, her face)

She's not getting it. It's mine. Wonder Woman saved
my life. She doesn't get to come in here, and waltz in
here, and . . . No. I control my own destiny.

Dramatic
The Inventor, forties

*The Inventor, in a fever-dream, envisions Wonder Woman
for the first time.*

THE INVENTOR: She's good, kind, powerful, all-seeing
. . . like a mother, the best kind of mother, she'll wrap
you in her strong embrace, pick you up off the floor
and cradle you. A woman strong enough to hold back
the demons, kiss your forehead, bring order and peace
to the world. Her legs are . . . powerful, seem to go
on forever, as you cling to the hem of her dress, bury
your face in her thighs. Look out at the world from
behind the silhouette of that powerful slope, those legs
leading up to the cradle of civilization, the source of life.
She's Lilith she's Inana she's Bathsheba she's mommy
reaching down absently to stroke your hair on the grocery store line, when you think you can't stand there
for one more minute and then she's touching you and
sweetness radiates down through your whole being and
you lean against that warm, powerful leg. She's Helen
she's Athena she's beauty and brains, she's got the smile
of the Mona Lisa 'cause she knows you'll never stop
wondering what it is she knows, and she knows she could
never quite explain, 'cause you don't know it, not yet,
but you will when you're grown. You will when you're
. . . Major Steve . . . . somebody. A fighting man, but
only fighting till the world is made right, till we can
have peace. She knows all and she sees all, she helps in
whatever ways she can, but she can't, always, sometimes
you have to figure things out for yourself. Sometimes
you have to hurt and mess up and hurt others and your
wife stares at you like—But she is watching over you,

she knows you're searching for something, something big, something vital, something that will change the very vibrations of the cosmos. She knows there's only so much a man can take before he needs to be hog-tied, that there's only so much worldly frustration he can have heaped on him before he needs those bonds to be made visible, tactile, something he can struggle against, biting into his skin. She understands everything you are, everything you think, everything you need. She is Betty Grable bending down to straighten a stocking and she is an Amazon Goddess slapping your stinging face for looking. She is strong, tall, powerful, beautiful, wise, knowing, on the side of right and good SHE IS

(he begins to sketch.)

Yes. Yes. She is . . . mine.

(looks up at us:)

Haven't you ever wanted to change the world?

Dramatic
Hogan, forties

Hogan is talking to a woman who rented his lakeside cabin during the previous summer with her kids, who has come back several months later to check up on him. She has heard that he almost drowned during the winter, and wants to know what happened. Hogan is a man who has had a lot of bad luck in his life, and who has made some bad decisions. He's also something of a liar, unwilling to confront the truth about himself. The truth is, his close call with death was no accident.

HOGAN: It was an accident. I admit it sounds a little silly now. I was trying to fix the dock. I always felt bad about not fully completing that project. And I was out here . . . I went through kind of I guess you'd call it a rough patch after last summer, you know, after you and your family had gone. I didn't stay here—it didn't seem wise, with all the tensions with my brother and sister-in-law, so there was a period there when I didn't have a firm base of operations, I was sort of floating more or less, you know, sleeping in the truck most nights. But I drove over here one day a couple weeks ago, gorgeous morning, just to check the place out, and it was so clear and sunny I just thought—there had been a little light snowfall the night before so even though the Lake only had the thinnest skin of ice on the surface it looked thick, with the snow resting on it, it looked like it used to look when we were kids and we could skate after a big freeze. I'm not an idiot. I knew I couldn't walk on it. I took the canoe. But it was such a gorgeous day—I don't know what it was like down in the city but up here it was gorgeous—I guess I just felt like this is the kind of day when you can do anything, you know. And maybe I was overambitious before, with the diving platform, but I've still got the lumber I bought, I can at least go out and replace some of the bad planks in the deck. It won't solve the pilings issue but maybe I can get us through another summer or two. I must have just slipped. The whole thing is sort of embarrassing in retrospect.

Information on this playwright may be found at:
www.smithandkraus.com.
Click on the WRITERS tab.

LOST LAKE
David Auburn

Dramatic
Hogan, forties

Hogan is a lost soul who lives in his truck while he rents out his cabin on a lake. He is talking to a woman from New York City who rented his cabin the previous summer, who has come back to check on him because she heard he almost drowned. Hogan's daughter refuses to have anything to do with him. She's started college in New York, and Hogan has this fantasy that he can just drive down there and see her and everything will be alright.

HOGAN: My daughter's at school there now, right? I was thinking about this the other day. What's to stop me getting in the truck and driving down? I don't have her contact information but she's in one of the dorms someplace. How many dorms could there be? She's on a soccer scholarship. It shouldn't be that hard to find the playing fields. Anyway, I could track her down and take her to lunch. *(Smiles)* I've got the cash. We could go someplace really upmarket. White tablecloth kind of thing. Actually, she's 18, she probably wouldn't want that. What do 18 year olds like? I'd hate for it just to be pizza. Whatever, that doesn't matter. I picture just surprising her on the street outside her dorm as she's coming in from practice. Like she turns a corner and I'm standing there and she stops and I just say "Can I buy you lunch?" And maybe it would be a little awkward at first. I mean of course it would be. Maybe she'd want to bring along a friend. That would be fine, if it would make her more comfortable. A couple friends. The more the merrier, long as I'm buying. You could even come. With your kids, I mean we'd have to coordinate a little bit, I'm not sure how that fits in with the rest of it, the spontaneous part, but we could get a big round table someplace like a Chinese restaurant, with the dishes in the middle and one of those spinning disks, what are they called? You can just turn it and everybody can help themselves to whatever they want.

Information on this playwright may be found at:
www.smithandkraus.com.
Click on the WRITERS tab.

Dramatic
Cal, mid to late forties

Cal's lover Andre died of AIDS. Now, twenty years later, Andre's mother has come for a visit. Here, he tells her what it was like during the early years of the AIDS epidemic.

CAL: I was in enough pain of my own. Andre was dying, I couldn't save him. Everyone was dying. I couldn't save any of them. Nothing could. Something was killing us. Something ugly. Everyone talked about it but no one did 45 anything. What would killing one another have accomplished? There was so much fear and anger in the face of so much death and no one was helping us. There wasn't time to hate. We learned to help each other, help each other in ways we never had before. It was the first time I ever felt a part of something, a community. So thank you for that, I suppose. I wanted to kill the world when Andre was diagnosed, but I took care of him instead. I bathed him, I cleaned him up and told him I loved him even when he was ashamed of what this disease had done to him. He wasn't very beautiful when he died, Mrs. Gerard. Our very own plague took care of that. Andre had slept with someone other than me but I had to forgive him. He was one of the unlucky ones. I'm not saying your son was promiscuous, Mrs. Gerard. But he wasn't faithful either. Monogamous. Of course we'd never taken marriage vows. We weren't allowed to. It wasn't even a possibility. Relationships like mine and Andre's weren't supposed to last. We didn't deserve the dignity of marriage. Maybe that's why AIDS happened.

Information on this playwright may be found at:
www.smithandkraus.com.
Click on the WRITERS tab.

Dramatic
Cal, mid to late forties

Cal's lover, Andre, died of AIDS. Now. Twenty years later, his mother has come for a visit. Cal tells of her of the anger he felt towards her during Andre's memorial.

CAL: You should have held me that day in the park. I'd lost Andre, too. Instead you made me feel ashamed and unwanted, just as you'd made Andre feel. We weren't strong then against people like you. You held all the cards. He wanted your love all his life, so much he had to pretend he didn't. So did I that day, God forgive me. I wanted you to love me for loving Andre. I wanted to forgive you. I don't anymore. I don't care. If you hadn't done this I wonder if I would have thought of you ever again. No offense, but I don't think news of your passing will make the *New York Times*, Mrs. Gerard. And then there truly will be none. It is sad when you think about it. But this thing isn't over. This thing that brought us all together and can still tear us apart. Young men are still falling in love but some of them are still being infected. And some of them are still dying. If anything like this happened to Bud—or Will, sure, there's that possibility, too—I would be devastated but I would not reject either one of them. I'm Will's husband, not his judge; Bud's father, not his scourge. If that were my son wasting, writhing, incoherent, incontinent in that bed in St. Vincent's, I would want him to know how much I loved him, how much I would always love him. I did what I could for Andre. I hope to this day it was enough.

Information on this playwright may be found at:
www.smithandkraus.com.
Click on the WRITERS tab.

Dramatic
Jan, late twenties-early thirties, white South African

Jan works for the government. His job is to make sure that inhabitants of Kliptown, Soweto used the materials the government provided them to rebuild their shacks after flooding in the area. He's very frustrated, because he has been walking around in the hot sun getting yelled at. Most of the people have sold the supplies or misused them, including a woman named Daweti who is dying of AIDS, who used some of her wood to build herself a coffin. This is direct address to the audience.

JAN: She built a fucking coffin! Ahhhhhhhhh!!!! This is my 12th house today. I use that term loosely, nothing I have seen today would I qualify as a home. A place where you put your heart, and keep it safe. You know. But every place I visited it's the same thing, "Get out! Hamba, hamba" little to no work done on improvements. Some of them didn't even have the supplies anymore. They probably sell them, who knows! They complain to their ANC Government, "You promised us this, you told us that. My house is flooded, Where is it?" Government actually sends them the supplies, which is a miracle in its self since the ANC never follows through on its promises, but they actually do for once and bam, sold or nothing done. Then they'll turn around next time it floods and ask for more. Complain about this and that. Everyone wants the quick fix, but they will do noth-ing for themselves. Even if you give it to them for free they won't build it. Waste of money. Worst part is that I don't give a shit about this job. I actually hate this job. Hate!! That's not a strong enough word. I don't want to care about what these people do with this shit. I studied philosophy like Plato, Kant, Marx, Hegel and Proudhon.

I debated over philosophy of poverty, the machinations of the state and the philosophy of right! "Man is born free but everywhere he is in chains"—Rousseau. I long for those conversations. The university is full of them. Then you leave and get some second rate job to pay the bills and they seem like a distant dream. Another reality on another planet. I can't even see them now. I think I have forgotten what I wanted to be or do in this world, like the sinew of my muscles are made up of hardship and pain, and disappointment, ahhh South Africa. It just seems pointless, like I'm striving and working to live in this shit . . . Jah, forget it. *(Pause)* I might just be clinically depressed. *(Beat)* I used to dream of such things like my mother or love, that electricity in an embrace, the dew on the trees in the early morning, and colors so many vibrant colors like you see only in the townships, ohh and rain, the smell of South Africa being washed clean. Now I have dreams of gunshots, but it's not just one shot it's many. I keep shooting, bam, bam, bam. On the last shot I wake! This shit job was one of the best I could get; all my friends said I was lucky, Ha!!! Affirmative action is for the black majority, 35 million blacks in this country, 5 million whites. I only got it because even the blacks didn't want to do it, going through townships asking people to prove they used the supplies from the government! White man, it's like a death wish! Jah, Jah, I know . . . nobody has pity for the crying Afrikaner, fathers of apartheid. But who are they when they turn around and do the exact same thing?

Information on this playwright may be found at:
www.smithandkraus.com.
Click on the WRITERS tab.

Dramatic
Meyerhold, thirties

The great Russian director Vsevolod Meyerhold has been working at the Moscow Art Theatre with its famous founder, Stanislavsky. But he has come to have very serious doubts about Stanislavsky's methods. While playing the role of a madman, and immersing himself deeply in the emotions of his character, as Stanislavsky taught, he has found himself terrified that he is actually going mad. This leads him to want to abandon psychological realism and emotion memory, and create instead a very different sort of theatre that employs a much more physical style of acting and an emphasis on a more external approach. He is finally venting his frustration to Stanislavsky here, just before leaving Stanislavsky's theatre and starting his own.

MEYERHOLD: I felt like I was going mad. You taught me to immerse myself in the emotion. And that's what I did. I felt the madman in me. And I don't want to be mad. And you pretend there's no audience. You can't act with integrity if you pretend there's no audience. If there's no audience, there's no theatre. The chemical reaction can only happen if you acknowledge, to yourself and to them that you know they're there. You tell them don't talk, don't smoke, don't crack nuts, don't make rude noises. Let them make all the noise they want. It's our job to get their attention. How can we blame them if we're the ones who aren't doing our job? Did we pay them to come? Do they work for us? No. We work for them. Or we all work together. To find something together. It's their theatre as much as ours. Leave the doors open. Let anybody in. Theatre should be a kind of beautifully controlled chaos. Like the music hall and the circus. Mystery plays, farces and carnivals. Dancing bears drinking vodka. Clowns.

There should be clowns everywhere. Experience comes to us in a jumble of strange fragments. And it's that strangeness out of which real art is made.

Dramatic
Brik, forty-two

Time: 1930. Osip Brik is a critic and champion of the Russian Revolution who has developed very close ties to the Cheka, the much feared Russian Secret Police. His wife Lily is the mistress of the great poet Mayakovsky, and Brik has apparently been very understanding about this. But in fact he has been assigned by the Cheka to keep an eye on the unpredictable Mayakovsky, and is in reality being eaten up inside by jealousy and hatred. Here his wife Lily has come home late and realized that Brik has been much more upset with her than she'd ever realized. What he is doing here, ultimately, is implying that if she doesn't start behaving the way he wants her to, he can have Mayakovsky killed at any time. He is a man with a tremendously repressed but very deep anger. He also, in his own twisted way, loves both Lily and Mayakovsky.

BRIK: Why would I be upset because the genius Mayakovsky is fucking my wife? He writes wonderful poetry and exciting plays and slogans for posters and he fucks my wife. Of course, I also fuck my wife, on rare occasions, at least once a year, when she's not busy, and sometimes when she's not there. But I write no poems. I write no plays. I write boring articles designed to prove that propaganda is art. I only connect to poetry through my wife when she's fucking the poet. Sometimes I have dreamed of choking you. Sooner or later the cuckoo comes out of the clock. Look over there, said Blok. Look the other way until you've forgotten what you love. While you have been out fucking the genius Mayakovsky all night, I have been having a wonderful time with my friends, the Secret Police. You and Mayakovsky should come along some evening. It's really very stimulating. To know that, at any moment, if you choose, you could have absolutely anybody arrested, interrogated, tortured, and killed for absolutely no reason at all. Absolutely anybody. *(Pause)* I want you. I'm not jealous any more, but I want you. Or, sometimes, I don't want you, but I'm jealous anyway. How absurd all this is. The illusion of love. The humiliation of desire. But the sages who advise us to renounce it are full of shit. Desire is all we have. I want you to swear to me that you will never leave me. That you will never, never leave me. Swear to me that whatever happens, you will never leave me.

Dramatic
Mayakovsky, thirties

Time: 1930 The great Russian poet and playwright Mayakovsky has been a champion of the Revolution and an enthusiastic supporter of the new Bolshevik government. He is a big man with a big personality, and he has been very enthusiastic about destroying everything old and replacing it with the new, including getting rid of all the great Russian writers of the past. But gradually he has become more and more disillusioned. Now that they're in power, the Bolsheviks want him to just write propaganda. His naturally rebellious spirit is making them nervous. And his mistress Lily Brik, whom he loves deeply, seems to be rejecting him and going back to her husband, who is an informer for the terrifying Secret Police who have been imprisoning and murdering writers. Here Mayakovsky, drinking and abandoned by Lily, his life's work now a joke, the flunky for a corrupt and repressive government, is expressing his frustration and despair to his friend Mandelstam.

MAYAKOVSKY: Shoot the clown in the head and cranberry juice comes squirting out. She is playing a sinister polka in my brain. A slap in the face of public taste. That's what I am. When did I become a flying prehistoric lizard? God help a poet who has outlived his usefulness. The world is leaking. The Devil is eating the moon. God lives at Luna Park. He's the fellow on stilts, with roller skates. Acrobats and roller coasters are the secret of life. I am the Jack of Diamonds and you are all playing cards. We are sailing to the island of the dead. Pushkin? Throw him overboard. Dostoyevsky? Overboard. Tolstoy? Overboard. Mayakovsky? Overboard. There is no room for them on this Ship of Fools. I don't care if those dumb fuckers are listening or not. I am the last poet. I'd rather be on the street selling pretzels than play their stupid game. These people have milked me like a cow. I am the bells on the dunce cap of God. They've got me writing advertisements for pacifiers. I made posters that said, There is nothing better for sucking. You can suck this until you're dead. This fellow who had such contempt for rules and regulations and hierarchies has become the poster boy for them. We are all dolls and puppets now. All that has become of our glorious revolution is a nation run by puppets under the head puppet, who is a homicidal maniac. I have been playing a character with my own name. What will happen to me when he dies?

Dramatic
Mandelstam, forties
Time: Late 1930s.

Osip Mandelstam, one of the great poets of the twentieth century, is a brilliant writer with a very dark sense of humor who has seen more clearly than his friends and fellow artists what a nightmare the Russian revolution is turning into. In the course of this play he has watched as one by one most of his friends, some of the greatest writers and artists of the century, are arrested, tortured, and either driven to suicide or murdered. Arrested, sent into exile, released and arrested again, he will ultimately be driven to the brink of madness and die on his way to a labor camp. But here, just before that, he tells his beloved friend and fellow poet Anna Akhmatova about his attempts to survive the nightmare they have all been living through.

MANDELSTAM I wake up in the middle of the night, absolutely certain Akhmatova has been arrested. It's the same way poems come to me. If I knew how they came, they wouldn't come. In my mind's eye, I have seen a corpse in the ravine. I must go out to the ravine to look for Akhmatova's corpse in the rain. But my wife talks me into coming back to bed. Nadezhda is tough. She says my jokes are going to get me killed. But I'll go mad if I stop making jokes. When I stop making jokes, that will be the day they've destroyed me utterly. Don't act like a clown, she says. But I am not the clown here. They'll drive us all mad. Khlebnikov carried his manuscripts around Petersburg in a pillowcase, following the birds, and starved to death. I have made things strange by making them impossibly complicated. But Stalin makes everything simple. There is life. There is death. There is death in life. There is life in death. The system selects for stupidity and mediocrity. It weeds out the truth tellers, drives them mad and kills them. My brain is a bag of dead hornets. Death crawling towards me like a spider. You take one streetcar. I'll take the other one. We'll see who dies first. Burn all your manuscripts but save what you scribbled in the margins. God is lurking in the marginalia. And save what you write in your dreams. I have studied the science of goodbyes. All the elegant mirage of Petersburg was a dream. Crawling up hill on our knees to Stalin. Painting birds on the walls in blood. The blood on the walls has not yet dried. All right, so I wrote a little poem about how Stalin was a homicidal maniac with fat fingers like grub worms and a mustache like a cockroach, and I happened to read it to a few friends. So he can't take a joke? Who knew?

Dramatic
Man, thirties to forties

A man explains how he got the world's record for seeing the most sunsets.

MAN: The first sunset . . . well, I was in my mother's arms and we were visiting Scotland and my father was still with us then. We'd just been walking for miles, me on my little legs and then on my father's shoulders when I got tired. See, my father was still with us then. It was so misty you could hardly tell day was ending. And of course this is a story that's been . . . well, told and retold so one can hardly tell the fact from the fiction . . . But we came to this break in the path, the path just stopped and my father who was still with us then and who was really very brave thought he'd jump over the break in the path and then give my mother and me a hand once he was on the other side. It was maybe a, well, a three or four foot ravine and we were getting hungry and the day was ending so there wasn't much thought. Turning back just didn't seem an option; it would take hours. So he jumped—my father—and we were watching because it seemed like a routine thing, because it was something he did without any fear. That's why when he fell it took a few moments just to believe it, to take it in; it's not easy to take in something that's going to change your life forever. So he fell and just like that my father wasn't with us anymore and my mother, after she took it all in, after she took in how far down the ravine went and how far he'd traveled just so we wouldn't waste a few hours while we were tired and hungry, cried aloud and I think, I mean, one could argue that when you see a parent cry—bang, childhood ends just like that. But for me, it was a different thing altogether; it was slower, I mean probably about fifteen minutes long and it happened half an hour or so later, when, walking back down the path, we saw the sun set.

Information on this playwright may be found at:
www.smithandkraus.com.
Click on the WRITERS tab.

Seriocomic
Lennie, seventeen to eighteen

*Lennie has sung "O Beautiful" at his school's talent show.
This is direct address to the audience.*

LENNIE: This is what I don't understand: why things come out of your mouth that you don't know why they're coming out of your mouth. Like, there's a person inside you, right, who's in charge. If that person isn't you then who is that person? And who is the one who thinks things like 'oh I'll just do this stupid thing and that will be fine.' Like, "O Beautiful"—like you think I'll sing this song, and it will be scary but kind of cool, a cool good thing to do. Honestly, like right now when I even just talk about it, it seems like such a stupid idea, such a colossally, who would ever think that that was a good idea? In what universe? And then when the words that come out aren't even the right words, its like whose idea was this and who is the person in here making up these words? In front of—you know, the whole—I mean it's like this: People say, high school sucks. And that sort of is supposed to make it okay, because everybody knows it sucks. And then you think when people say that, what they think they mean is that high school sucks but the rest of life is going to be okay. Isn't that what that means? But then you look around and go high school doesn't actually suck for everyone, why can't I be one of the people it doesn't suck for? Because sometimes when I'm doing my homework— or I look around and there's a person who's—and you think wow, this could be great. But maybe knowing that is sort of like knowing the words to "O Beautiful." I mean the fact is maybe you don't, maybe you don't know them at all.

*Information on this playwright may be found at:
www.smithandkraus.com. Click on the WRITERS tab.*

Dramatic
Lennie, seventeen to eighteen

Lennie, a high school student, addresses the audience.

LENNIE Your brain is so weird. Like, you're thinking something and then you feel something and you totally forget what you were thinking in the first place. And then you remember it again like the next day, like where did that go, and then why did it come back? Are the things you think real, even, if they can disappear like that? Because there's you and there's your brain and then there's the thing your brain thinks and if you wrote it down before you forgot it, it would be outside of you, like on a piece of paper. So it would be real then, but not if you don't write it down? Because writing is just writing, it's not the thing you're writing about, those are two different things. I like thinking about questions, my brain is happy when it thinks things. So you would think I mean I would think that because you're happy your brain would want to stay there and just stay happy but then it's like this other part of you comes along and just wrecks everything. And it's like IN you, like IN your brain but then you know, like, really, it's like you're having an argument with yourself and there's a couple of people in there. But that's, okay look that's totally, I'm not saying you're like a multiple personality or anything; that's not what I'm talking about. Although I would like to meet someone with multiple personalities, that sounds kind of interesting to me. Unless some of them were mean to the other ones. That wouldn't be so good. To have a mean person in*side* you? Because when people are mean that really is what makes the ideas—that make you happy—it makes them disappear.

Information on this playwright may be found at:
www.smithandkraus.com. Click on the WRITERS tab.

A Particle of Dread (Oedipus Variations)
Sam Shepard

Dramatic
Uncle Del, fifties

*Uncle Del knows the truth about the murders of the king and
two companions, and the dire consequences for the murderer,
the queen, and the country. The play is a brilliant riff on the
Oepidus story. This is a direct address to the audience.*

UNCLE DEL: What began it all, that's the question. I'll tell you
what it is. You want to know? It's simple. But simple things
are sometimes the hardest to hear, aren't they? Murder.
Yes. That's what started this curse on our city. This disease.
Plague. Epidemic. Murder. Plain and simple. Right here—
Years ago, just outside of town. Deserted highway. Desert.
No wind, to speak of. The bodies were all in pieces. The
heads here. Arms and legs over there. They had to search for
all the parts. The King's penis was missing. Imagine that!
Some crow or coyote must have got it. Vandals maybe. No
matter. They put the bodies back together. Laid them out
like a jigsaw puzzle. The King. That's what he was. Back
when Kings were Kings. They say a band of bandits way-
laid him—outnumbered and overwhelmed him. Others say
a single man was the culprit. Ran him over with his own
carriage. Scattered his parts and vanished. Now it's clear
this murder has brought the trouble on us. An old defile-
ment we may be sheltering. He's here among us now, this
killer. Snickering at our misery. Slithering between our feet.
Daring us to expose him — bring him into the light of day.
Until we uncover this vermin we will continue to suffer our
slow and painful disintegration. But who among you fears
they'll find him in their own dark kitchen?

*Information on this playwright may be found at:
www.smithandkraus.com. Click on the WRITERS tab.*

Dramatic
Maniac of the Outskirts, any age

*The Maniac is a homeless man who inhabits the desert.
This is direct address to the audience.*

MANIAC You! You think it's possible to hide from me? Have you got any vague notion who I am? Who I'm intended to be? I thought not. Just another vagabond I suppose. Invisible. Lost through the cracks. Little do you realize—Have you any idea whatsoever who you're dealing with? Where I come from? My powerful lineage? My father—My father, for instance, had one of the largest, most expansive Chevy dealerships in the entire county of San Bernardino! That surprises you, doesn't it? Takes you back some. The whole stinking county! Sold more Chevys than ten men over those decades. Those early decades when Chevy was King! Just hitting its stride with the fins and all. Chrome! You never saw chrome like that! Bumpers flashing—Hood ornaments parading—back when steel ruled the universe! Detroit in all its glory! A shining beacon. Passed you by like dust in the rearview mirror, didn't it! Dust! Well, just remember one thing—I am not anonymous. I am not going to just crumble away into oblivion. I will live forever! Don't forget that. Don't forget that.

*Information on this playwright may be found at:
www.smithandkraus.com.
Click on the WRITERS tab.*

Dramatic
Oedipus, late forties to fifties

In this brilliant riff on the Oedipus tale, the police have reopened the cold case of the murder of the king and 2 companions. Oedipus, now the king is determined to find the killer. Little does he know, it's him. This is direct address to the audience.

OEDIPUS: Until now I was a stranger to this tale. A stranger to the crime. How could this be? All this time lurking among us like the slinking dogs, from corpse to corpse. Any common day I could have brushed up against him in the marketplace. Seen him eye to eye. Not knowing. Even now he could have the audacity to be sitting right here amongst us. Inwardly sneering in our midst. Licking his chops like the green-eyed hyena. Let me tell you that if anyone here has the slightest suspicion who might have been the killer, or worse—may be harboring this demon, let him come forward and surrender with the promise that no further tribulation will come to him. Banishment will occur in utter safety. Know also that I solemnly forbid anyone to receive this man or speak to him, no matter who he pretends to be in the community. He must be driven from every house, every nesting place; shunned as you've shunned the plague bearers akin to you. I pray that this man's life be consumed in evil and wretchedness. And I vouch that this curse applies no less to me, should it turn out that somehow he has conned his way into my company; sharing my family and hearth. I now take the son's part in this revenge as though the King were my own blood father. I will see this thing through to the naked end.

Information on this playwright may be found at:
www.smithandkraus.com.
Click on the WRITERS tab.

Cori Thomas

Dramatic
Femor, fourteen, Liberian

Femor, a child soldier in Liberia, is threatening Cora, whom he has arrested on suspicion of spying, with a "sassywood trial." A sassywood trial is a trial by ordeal to scope out criminals. A person is made to put their hand in hot oil or such as described in the monologue to see if they are telling the truth.

FEMOR: Sassywood man playing a trick on her to see if she tell true, O. If she tell true, she can't die. No matter what trick they try, they can't hurt her. If Sassywood man put her hand in oil she can't burn. Or sometimes they use switch or cutlass. One time I see them doing it with switch. One man start to beat the drum. Boom, boom boom. Sassywood man, shake the switch, wo wo wo, the switch push him so he jump. Wo. *(showing how the Sassywood man twitches)* It move him straight to the liar. All the people from that house they standing in one straight line. He testing them one by one. If they innocent, they stand straight, they can't be afraid. Because they na do nothing, O. When he come to the the one who the wrong one, ehehnh! He begin to sweat, O. Wo wo the switch almost jump from his hand. And the one who lie begin to cry, "Wah Wah don't beat me, O. I sorry ya? Don't beat me, O." Ehehnh! Because by now he know Sassywood switch will beat him good. Pa's Hat: Liberian Legacy This woman lying, that's why she can burn and die. She say she fighting for God, she na fighting for no God, O. Your head na rise up and you think you know some big big something, and I ehn know nothing, but you ehn know nothing too, O. If Sassywood ask me did I kill someone. I will answer for true. I will say yes Sassywood Man, I kill people. In time of war, people got to die. But you not the same way woman, when the time of the trial come, you will die, or you will suffer, like that woman. She dying, eneh so? Read and write, and France. Shucks, that thing can't do nothing in time of war. That thing ehn for true, O. It can't make you nothing. It can't make you strong and stay alive. It can't give you no food to put inside your stomach. I don't read no book right now to this time, I can't read no words inside my small small bible. But I pray like my Ma teach me. And one day God sending me my hair and my shades. What he sending you? If Sassywood man putting the hot cutlass on you, I think it will burn you, eneh so?

Information on this playwright may be found at:
www.smithandkraus.com.
Click on the WRITERS tab.

Dramatic
Jimmy, forty-four

In 1941, Jimmy Casey, 44, is sitting with his twelve year old niece, Dolly, who's come to him looking for a home, watching her eat a big sandwich. He doesn't know what to do with her, and is not sure how to talk to her. Jimmy has been a soldier in the First World War, and now repairs cars, clocks, and especially old pianos, and plays the piano at a local beer joint sometimes. He is lonely and lost and closed up with grief after the death of Jessie, who he loved very much. But Dolly has always loved to sit outside the window and listen to him play the piano, and she has just asked him how he got so good at it. In trying to answer her, he is opening up to her for the first time in his life, on a subject that means a lot to him.

JIMMY: When I was a kid, I used to go hang out in the bushes behind Mrs Unkefer's house, and listen to her give music lessons to the MacBeth sisters. They were awful. They really couldn't play at all. I don't know how Mrs. Unkefer stood it. No matter how much they practiced, they just didn't have a good feeling for it, you know? But then she'd sit down to play. I guess she wasn't all that great, either, really, but at least she hit all the right notes. I knew how it should sound. I just knew, in my head. And one day she went to the grocery store, it was a hot summer day, and she left her door open, just the screen door, not latched or anything, and I just couldn't help myself any more. I snuck into her house and sat down at her piano and started to play. I couldn't play it right, of course. But I could pick out the tune of this Chopin piece I'd heard her play. I was kind of in a trance, to be making any kind of music. I just forgot about everything else. I don't know how long I was there, but when I got to the end of the song, all of a sudden I kind of woke up out of the trance, and I knew I wasn't alone in the room any more, and I turned around and there was Mrs. Unkefer, standing on the rug behind me, with a bag of groceries in her hand, and her mouth open, staring at me. I'm sorry, I said. The door was open. I'm sorry. And I got up and started to run out past her. But she called me back. I can still hear her voice—kind of school teachery, and no nonsense. It stopped me dead in my tracks. Jimmy Casey, she said, you get back here. So I turned around and walked back to her, and my knees were shaking so bad I could hardly walk. And then she put down her grocery bag on the rug and kneeled down and looked me in the eye and said, Jimmy, who taught you to play the piano like that? And I said, nobody. I just mess around sometimes on Uncle Willy's old pianos in the barn. And she said, but how did you learn to play that song? And I said, I listen sometimes, when you're playing. And she looked at me, and she thought about it a minute, and then she said, Jimmy, would you like me to give you lessons, sometimes? And I told her thank you, but I didn't think we couldn't afford that, and Mama and Papa didn't much like pianos anyway, and they thought my Uncle Willy was crazy for filling up his barn with them. But she said, Jimmy, you have a gift. And it's a sin to waste a gift. If you have a gift, you need to treasure it, and nurture it, so you can give to others. And she let me come by every day after that, and she taught me how to read music, and we played Chopin and Beethoven and Bach and Mozart. And then one day when Uncle Willy heard me playing Beethoven on one of his old pianos, he started to cry, and he said, Jimmy, when I die, I'm going to give you my barn full of pianos. And he did.

Information on this playwright may be found at:
www.smithandkraus.com.
Click on the WRITERS tab.

Dramatic
Jimmy, thirty-one

1928. Jimmy Casey has gone to Hollywood to kill John Rose, an actor in silent movies, because John has committed incest with his sister Jessie and impregnated her, and Jessie later died. Jimmy was deeply in love with Jessie, and blames Jessie's brother John for the incestuous relationship that led to her death. He finds John drinking in an alley in Hollywood late at night. John has been waiting for him, and, in despair himself, calmly invites Jimmy to kill him. But Jimmy can't do it. Like John, he's been a soldier, and has shown himself capable of violence in the past, but here he finally admits to John the truth that's been eating him up inside, that Jimmy himself feels responsible for Jessie's death.

JIMMY: She wanted to go out dancing. I told her it was too soon after she had the baby. Doc Wolf told her to stay in bed for a while. Your mother told her. Sarah told her. Lizzie told her. Everybody told her. But Jessie said she just had to get out of there. She begged me to take her out dancing. I said no, I wouldn't do it, but she kept after me. You know how she was. And I just couldn't say no to her. I never could say no to her. I couldn't stand for her to be unhappy or disappointed. And I couldn't stand to be away from her. I tried, but I couldn't. I kept coming back to her. Even after I knew she was pregnant, even after I knew who the father had to be, I still couldn't stay away from her. To be out with Jessie, driving in the night down dark roads. I'd have given anything for that. Just to have her there beside me, nestled under my arm, trusting me. I'd have signed away my soul for that. Anything. When I was alone, she was all I could think about. She was always there in my head. She's still there. I couldn't say no. And I didn't want her going out with anybody else. So I drove up there in the dark to that big old monstrous haunted house you people were raised in, and snuck her out of there, and we went dancing, like she wanted. She was so beautiful that night. That was the night she started to hemorrhage and it wouldn't stop. Because I couldn't say no to her, even when it was for her own good. It was me. It was my fault. I couldn't deny her anything. And that's why she's dead.

Dramatic
Frank, fifties, African-American

FRANK: is a former NFL star, now retired. He has agreed to appear on TV with another former NFL player, whom he put in a wheelchair for life with one hit. He is talking to the producer, an African-American man in his 30s. He has asked him who his favorite player was when he was a kid. FRANK. See, I'd feel you if you'd said Joe Greene or Franco Harris. But Terry Fucking Bradshaw? Get the fuck out of here. I mean, not only was he a cracker, but he tried too fucking hard to be liked. I played against the motherfucker—always out there signing autographs, waving to the fans, grinnin' that dumb-ass Louisiana grin. Not me. Game day came: I had focus. I didn't have no time for sideline theatrics. You've got to keep your eyes open out there, or you'll get wrecked. Shit, you'll get wrecked anyway—one way or another. Eat or be eaten, that's right! And on the football field, you got a license to kill. Who needs knives and pistols anymore? I say ban them all; give everybody a helmet and a pair of cleats. But see, the rules have all changed. It's not like it was. The game's been tainted by these watereddown rules. I mean, no roughing the passer? Don't hit the receiver while he's in mid-air? What's that all about? See, what you're talking about is the line. Between taking a man down and putting him down—permanently. Tell me where it is and then we can talk. From a young age they train you do something and then suddenly it's out of bounds. All I know how to do is play—to grab, to tackle, to smash, to stomp. I can't tell you about the physics of the thing—you know, bodies in motion, rates of acceleration, mass over whatever the fuck they use to calculate impact. The thing is, once you cross that invisible line between being hurt and being injured—the one nobody can seem to locate—they say, "Oh, you went too far. You're a bad man. You have to be punished." But what I want to know is, where is that line exactly?

Dramatic
Lewis, thirties, African-American

Lewis, a TV producer, has arranged for two former NFL players to appear together on camera to talk about a notorious moment years ago when one player put the other in a wheelchair for life with one hit during a game. He is talking to Frank Baker, the player who made the hit. It turns out, the player he hit was his father. Lewis blames himself for what happened.

LEWIS: You were my hero, Frank. Bradshaw was nothing compared to you. You had the tight mustache, the badass 'fro, and you didn't take shit from anybody. Hell no, man, you doled it out like poison candy. And those uniforms: The silver and black, the pirate logo on the helmet. What little kid doesn't want to be a pirate, right? My father brought home Patriot merchandise all the time, but I didn't want it. Finally, he gave in and for my birthday he bought me your jersey with the number 32 and B-A-K-E-R spelled out between the back shoulders. I wore it for three weeks straight; I slept in the Goddamn thing. They couldn't get it off of me. Two months later I was wearing it on the sidelines of a preseason game between the New England Patriots and the Oakland Raiders. It was only an exhibition game—it was meaningless—but it was the only game I cared about. You know why? Because I knew you would be there. My father told me he didn't know you very well, but he said he'd try to introduce the two of us when it was over. He never got the chance. I had the jersey on in the ambulance on the way to the hospital. Nobody paid any attention; I forgot I was wearing it until my mother took me home that night. We got in the front door and suddenly she was just standing there, looking at me. "Take that off," she said. I didn't know what she meant. She slapped me across the face. "Take it off, I said!" I took it off, and then it was gone. I wanted to hate you, but I couldn't. So I hated myself. Jesus, I'd been raised to love the game for what it was: the bigger the plays, the harder the hitting— the better. See, football gave my father a life—opportunities beyond anything a black man in the '70s could have ever dreamed of. I betrayed him. And all those years I wiped his ass, brushed his teeth, got him dressed—all those years my mother struggled to feed us, keep a roof over our heads—the only thing I could think about was how things would have been different if only I hadn't . . . He always wanted me to go to Howard, like he had. I went for a semester, but after my mother died . . . well, I was the only one left to care for him. I couldn't just abandon him could I? And now with the contract and the book, well, I could say, "Look, pop, look what I did. Look what I did for you, for us. I got Frank Baker to take responsibility for what happened, and to say that's he's sorry too. It can't be my fault— what happened to you, pop. It can't be my fault."

Theresa Rebeck

Dramatic
Ian, thirties to forties, Irish

Ian is a guest for the weekend at Ella and Peter's country house. Ella believes strongly that "beauty" is an objective concept. She's a romantic. Ian is a total cynic. She has cited Yosemite Valley as an example of something that is beautiful. Ian disagrees.

IAN: Listen. Yosemite Valley's spiritual value to the native Americans of the Sierra Nevada caused them to shroud its existence from the barbarians, your forefathers, until finally a couple of the worst of those tribes did something stupid, they chopped up one or two aforementioned settlers, and so the military was sent after these renegade fools, and they fled into the high sierra where they thought they would be safe because no one knew about that so called holy valley, but the well-armed regiment that was sent after them found that valley, didn't they, and then they slaughtered everyone who lived there and most of these brilliant military men didn't even look at it. They were too busy killing people to see it, this spectacularly magnificent hand of God valley went completely unnoticed by all of them! But one. One benighted officer who in the middle of the bloodshed did look around and think my god this is fantastic and he wrote back to his friends in the east and said you know you've got to see it and that spawned a train of tourists which today crowds the roads and poisons the air of that apocalyptic fantasyland, so no. I do not think the word "beautiful" covers, precisely, what Yosemite Valley is.

Dramatic
Ian, thirties to forties, Irish

Ian and his wife Maureen are weekend guests at the country house of Peter and Ella. Ian and Maureen have had a huge row, at the end of which she has accused him of having an affair with Ella. Then, she has told Peter about this affair. He doesn't believe it, but doesn't want to be caught up in whatever's going on with Ian and Maureen, so he has asked Ian to leave.

IAN: You're asking me to leave. Why? Because my wife told you something? My wife who everyone knows is completely raving bonkers, the woman is an emotional lunatic from start to finish, you told me yourself, at our engagement party, the night we were celebrating our engagement you were drunk and you said to me that you've known her your entire life and you think she's crackers. You were nice enough about it as you always are, Americans are always so nice about things. Not all of you, but those of you from the middle part of the country, all those states with all the farmland, polite to a fault every last one of you, when you're not waving banners and screaming like lunatics, it's as if all that farmland bores you to death or drives you insane. I'm making a really good point here. You had actually just arrived, you had just taken that job in the city and Maureen insisted we invite you, I didn't even know you but that whole thing with your brother, who was at the time still carrying a torch if Maureen was to be believed—I'm told we've GOT to invite you because of your poor sad lovesick brother, I don't know you and I could give a shit about your brother, frankly, I've just got engaged to a woman who at the time I found honestly delightful, I did, I was in love with her and America too, truth be told, why not,

America looks great when you're young and sick of Europe, which I was, all that fucking history, seriously you really do get worn out, it's so calcified. And of course the middle of your country hadn't gone insane yet so you just looked—beautiful. So cheers, I'm going to marry a terrific American girl, we're toasting to my upcoming nuptials in some total stranger's kitchen and you just blurt it, you come out and tell me in no uncertain terms that I will regret marrying her because she's a lunatic. And I married her anyway and you're right, she's insane, and we've talked about it many times since, you and I, over drinks, at dinners and cocktail parties, never so explicitly, "how is it being married to that completely insane woman, you know I warned you!" More subtle than that but not all that subtle. But it's always in the air, too bad for Ian, married to that woman, you've always been really rather smug about it truth be told. No you have! Because you have Ella. And I have Maureen. Which always made me wonder. When she'd come home and say, oh guess what good news Peter and Ella have asked us up to their house for the weekend, won't that be grand. The question really is grand for whom?

Dramatic
Ian, thirties to forties, Irish

*Ian and his wife Maureen are weekend guests at the country
home of Ella and Peter. Maureen is distraught because she
thinks Ian and Ella are having an affair. By this point, Ian
has had enough of her crazy accusations.*

IAN: You really are just mad as a hatter. And I say that with
love, as much love as I have left after all this time. Peter
was right, when he mentioned it at that party, I didn't
see it then because you know for all those paranoid
suspicions you hoard and nurture you've quite forgotten
the possibility that I was in love with you. Honestly I
thought you were exquisite, and fun, darling, you really
were, you were—well, what does it matter. He was right;
I was wrong; turns out you're completely crackers. I'm
not saying that I think you're about to hole up in a clock
tower somewhere and start picking off undergraduates,
one at a time or you know I don't believe you're in psy-
chic communication with creatures from another galaxy.
But you are just barking, well what is insanity, you have
to ask yourself. When so many things, that vast unreason,
or non reason at the center of so much of what we face
every day, we know it's there, it plagues us, the thought
that reality itself truly might just be mad, the daily
journey from dawn to dusk carrying with it finally too
many—too much—Christ, God knows there's theories
about all of it, whole books about the workings of power
and love and science and history but they none of them
ever I think explain the essential—disappointment—of
living with so much insulting irrationality. Over time. So
many people appearing sane and then they say something
or do something, God, the sudden revelation of an inte-
rior life that is completely well more than indefensible,

how many times are we supposed to accept the terror of daily—and not only that. Or not even. Because the real indignity, finally, is that crashingly horrifying discovery that your soul was wrong. Was in fact just stupid, your soul, and how do you live with that, how do you live with the utter insult of cataclysmic personal mistakes? Well we do. We just make do, God help us; we content ourselves with the memory of a hope that it is possible, perhaps to occasionally, at random, encounter a shred of subjectivity that somehow lives in relation to your shred, there's something else out there that for a moment might recognize—you. The thing that is just you, in your essence. Might be seen. By another shred. And the hope of that possibility calms you just enough to put up with the everyday madness and that helps you get used to it, doesn't it. Hope sustains us just enough actually, so that insanity—you know, the real thing, insanity—doesn't seem quite so dramatic. It's just the sea we swim in. It's just your wife. It's just you, darling. It's you.

Dramatic
Ian, thirties to forties, Irish

Ian and his wife Maureen are weekend guests at the home of Ella and Peter. Maureen has accused Ian of having an affair with Ella, and has told Peter about it. All hell ensues. Ella believes in the institution of marriage. Ian fervently disagrees with her. This is part of their larger debate about the concept of "good."

IAN: Why do Americans persist in thinking that it is "moral" and "good" to remain addicted to an institution which has driven them mad? You all think the most insane and dangerous leaders imaginable are decent as long as they're in a supposedly sound marriage. The holiness of marriage is your security blanket, it's the fog you wrap yourselves in so you can destroy yourselves without thinking about it. No, don't try to argue with me about this; that's not a debatable point. Everyone on the planet is talking about it. We're crushed, honestly. Do you think we weren't rooting for you? Because we were. You were our dream. And then you threw it away, you threw away the Enlightenment, for what? For marriage? I'm telling you, the entire planet is crushed. And trust me, we're seriously sick of the whole goodness thing too. No matter what sort of catastrophe you get yourselves involved in, you still need to see yourselves as good. How can we be good? Let's see. I can be nice. Americans like to be nice. I can eat a lot. I don't know if that makes you good but it seems to calm people down. I can make a lot of money, well that's a fascination to everyone, old world or new. Oh, and then there's the children! Those innately good children, to whom we will leave a world so corrupt and vulgar it's truly terrifying to contemplate. Well, we don't have to think about that one, you and I avoided that particular deception. But seriously. Doesn't it finally lead you to the real question: If goodness is just an anaesthetic is it still goodness? Especially if anaesthesia isn't finally just an excuse to release the worst in us. Our own little excuse for poor behavior.

POZ (+)
Michael Aman

Dramatic
Arthur, thirties

Arthur is a stunningly beautiful man—a bit flamboyant. In his thirties—at least he looks like he is because that's how old he was when he died. His fashion shows that he's stuck in 1991. In the monologue, Arthur is speaking to his dear friend Red who still mourns for him a dozen years since he passed. She can't see him, but somehow she senses he is there and that is why he speaks to her. He wants to pull her out of her reverie. Red is fearful that the young man she has grown fond of will die much like Arthur did and Arthur is trying to comfort her.

ARTHUR: Remember in 1989 when I was in that piece that was going to be my debut at the Joyce Theatre—the one that was canceled? My dancing partner was this tiny ballerina monster who condescended to perform in a contemporary dance piece. In rehearsals she and I were developing this motif that involved a series of *pas de chat.* A crack in my toe started bleeding and the room became frozen. Neither of us realized what had happened, but we could sense the energy shift. I looked down at my toe and she followed my gaze. The trail of blood led from my toe to her bare foot. Those days everyone had assumptions about me. I had lost weight. I had missed work. They were right of course. When she saw the blood, I no longer existed. Poof. Arthur is gone. She started yelling at the choreographer—a young Belgian who was completely overwhelmed. She pointed at me as if I was the car that hit her. She grabbed a water bottle and poured water all over her foot. She threw the bottle at me and left. And through the whole thing nobody said a word. It was creepy. That's why the show was canceled. I couldn't tell you. But you knew. That's why I always kiss you, Red. Even though you don't feel it. You'll understand someday. Maia's right. It doesn't end. The closest I came to it back then was when I would leap. Remember? In white tights or black? Oh! The way I looked in those tights—my basket was as big and round as my granite ass. I'd get my musical cue and I'd leave the ground on great springs in my legs and for that second or two I was in the air I was no longer stuck. I turned into sparkle. That's what you called it. Like when you dissolved on stage as Kate or Martha or Julie. Sparkle. Like those shoes I bought you on St. Mark's Place. Or that dress I wore at the parade. "The Dying Diva." I didn't know I was addicted to breathing—just like you. Red, those two seconds in the air last forever. The touchy-fingery physical stuff is just temporary. Don't worry about the boy. Go back to what you're meant to be. Be airborn. Dissolve.

Information on this playwright may be found at:
www.smithandkraus.com.
Click on the WRITERS tab.

Seriocomic
Daizy, twenties

Daizy is talking to his friend Emily, who makes dolls.

DAIZY: I fucking hate dolls, you know? I don't get the appeal, to be honest with you. I was completely gay as a six-year-old. Listened to "Free to Be" all the time. I wanted a Cabbage Patch Kid, more than anything. I got one. My dad went out, fought off the Christmas hordes, brought me home an African-American "Preemie" named Tabitha. To encourage diversity. I had no idea what to do with her. This thing. She looked nothing like me. I couldn't make a connection. My friend Arthur? He got a boy doll. With a cowboy hat and a lasso. Named Dennis. It was completely fucking awesome. I shaved off all of Tabitha's hair. Mom made her a leather jacket and sparkly glove, circa "Bad," which I thought was pretty fucking macho, and . . . I tried to like her. I tried, y'know? I pretended she was like me on the inside, just trapped. In that lady-body. Poor Tabitha was the world's first passing tranny butch self-loathing Cabbage Patch doll. My parents were horrified. Their son, the racist, sexist, six-year-old. Eventually they gave in. I switched to G.I. Joe, you know. He-Man. Man-Tech. Action figures. So now I'm sculpting dicks for a living. Go figure. My point is, I guess I know how . . . *intense* people can feel— about these things. I mean—I don't want to trivialize. What you're going through . . . *But*, yeah . . . I mean, you seem like a sensible adult. A successful—lawyer or whatever you are? Why Kelly? Why dolls? What the fuck happened to you?

Dramatic
Chuck, sixty-three, African-American

Charles "Chuck" Davis, Jr. is the CEO of Davis Janitorial in the suburbs of Tulsa, OK. Chuck, on the brink of retirement, looks to secure a positive legacy for his company and family name. In this scene Chuck warns his first cousin Lois' son, Seth—a 23 year old first-year law student who has lived with Chuck and his wife since middle school—about the dangers of getting involved in Lois' reparations quest.

CHUCK: I ain't gon' be in trouble. Anna cain't see. She nice to a fault. All she see is the surface. She take it for face value. She don't look into nothin'. She ain't got no history with yo' mama. Not like I do. 'Cause if she did . . .! ! Wanna know what one of my first memories of life was? I remember being at my granddaddy's house. It was when he had just been made head janitor, before he went and got his own thing, and for some holiday he was invited to the white folks ranch to rub elbows. So we was all going, my mom and dad, lil' cousin Lois and her father, my uncle Rufus, wives, everybody. We get there and this man has everything on his ranch—horses and even some bulls for riding later on. I remember everything being so sunny and so hot I could feel the heat from the ground through my sandals. To keep us cool the white man had the best lemonade I ever tasted and he had made a sprinkler system for his kids that rained down into a big chili bowl lookin' thing, so that when the sprinklers needed to get cut off, when the water ran out, we could still play in the pool of accumulated water. That white man was real nice, I remember him smiling at me, laughing with my granddaddy, talking to him like a man, like a friend. But nice as that man was, he had some devil off-spring. They made it known that they knew we was black and that black was the worse thing a person could be. And they made it real clear that they didn't want us to be in the water with them. One of 'em even tried to wash the black off my cousin Curtis, so that well into high school Curtis still wouldn't stand in the sun too long for fear of getting blacker. But as long as they daddy was 'round, they couldn't kick us out. They had to deal with it, and we could stay cool while the adults was elbow rubbin'. And then Lois, I'll never forget this, Lois got real still in the pool. Everybody was splashing and laughing, and she just stood there real still, and a band of yellow started to grow around her while she sat there in the middle of the bowl. And that little devil white boy started yellin', "The nigger gal peed in the pool! The nigger gal peed in the pool!!" Everybody run over to see 'bout the commotion, and they pull us out, the white ladies lookin' mortified that they little boys, the next big oil tycoons, was sittin' in the pool of nigger pee. And my grandaddy looks to my uncle Rufus, to say something, to apologize, and he say that she just a little girl and don't know no better, but he don't say sorry. He don't say nothin'. I remember that white man loosen his smile, so that he look just like the older version of his satan kids. He looked at me, right at me, like I was just like Lois! Like I had done the peeing! My granddaddy rounded us all up and we left. We had to leave 'cause we was all associated to the piss! Everything yo' mama touch go to hell in a wastebasket. Don't let her pull you into this reparations nonsense, cause . . . Mark my words, you keep her 'round you long enough, she'll pee in your pool too.

Dramatic
Seth, twenty-three, African-American

Seth Sanders is a first-year law student at NYU. He has re-
turned home to his native Tulsa, OK to celebrate the holiday
season, with the full intention of disappointing his family
with news that he planned to return to NYC for New Year's
Eve. His plans are thwarted when his mother-figure, Anna,
invites his ex-girlfriend, Debbie, to the family's festivities.
In this scene Seth explains to Debbie why he doesn't want
to get invested in his mother's quest for reparations.

SETH: I'm just remembering . . . *(beat)* When I. . . When I
was a kid I used to make believe my mom was secretly
rich. I used to pretend that secretly she was super duper
rich, and that she had such a hard time getting people
to love her for her and not for her money that she pretended to be loud, and rude and uncouth and broke
down and poor. To test people's intentions. But secretly
she was like Clair Huxtable, right? And I pretended I
was pretending to be a poor kid with rags for clothes,
but underneath, I was really just like Theo. And our life
was really like one of those episodes of the Cosby Show
where everybody pretended to be all hard-core to teach
Theo—to teach me—a lesson. So, she raised me poor
to make sure I was a man of character, you know, that I
would have morals. That I would be a good person. That
I knew the value of a dollar. And she could've paid for
all my schools—for Briarwood Academy, U of O—for
all of 'em, upfront if she needed to. But she wanted me
to appreciate my education, so she made me work hard
to earn scholarships. And she sent me away to live here.
. . .she sent me away to stay with Anna and Chuck so
that I'd learn independence. She didn't want me to be
like those snot-nosed, mama's boys with silver-spoons in

their mouths that thought the world was made for them. So I thought that, once I proved that I wasn't like them, that I was a good person—I made good grades and really turned out to be someone, she would shed her skin or something and finally reveal that she was filthy rich and bestow upon me this enormous inheritance. 'Cause I had proved I was worthy. I passed the test. And we'd live happily ever after. *(beat)* And, silly as it may sound, the day after graduation day, she slept on the couch. And this part of me still expected the metamorphosis to occur. For her to morph into Glinda the good witch and sing a song or something and finally release me from . . . . But I sat there watching her sleep. I just watched her. She was snoring. Loud. She had always snored, but she was particularly loud. And I looked at her. Her mouth all wide open. Her chest working real hard to get air—and I realized that when she woke up . . . *(Lois wakes up)* I realized there wasn't going to be any transformation. She would never change. No matter how hard I worked. Nothing I did would . . . If anything, I'd wake up 25 years from now still in Tulsa watching her snore on the couch in cousin Chuck's living room. And I finally said to myself —I think I even said it out loud—I gave myself like this intervention looking in the bathroom mirror and I said, "There is. No. Inheritance." *(beat)* It was just a dream I held onto to help me . . . An irrational . . . hallucination I held on to for much too long. I have lived for 22 years on that dream. Hoping she was. . . Hoping I could push her, pull us . . . *(beat)* But I can't. She doesn't want to go. And I don't wanna stay. I want my life to be . . . . In New York, nobody even knows what the Tulsa Race Riot was or that it ever existed. They don't know where Tulsa is. They don't know where Greenwood is or what it means. And they don't care. I am whoever I say I am. And I can be whatever I want to be. I don't represent anything. I don't have to stand up for anything. I'm not associated with anyone. I can just be. Me.

Comic
Ethan, twenty-eight

Ethan has written two NY Times best sellers, based on his blog. Here he tells Olivia, who has published one not very successful novel, about his books.

ETHAN: The blog was getting over a million hits a month, mostly from people under twenty-five. The tasteless youth of the world put me on the Best Seller list! And that's why critics haven't liked me. They all want to be king-makers, hanging on to their last bit of power before their papers went under. But so many of those guys don't have jobs anymore, which is some sweet satisfaction. But, in the end, they didn't matter anyway. I got totally mixed reviews and I was on the Best Seller list for five years! And even though I've been off that for a year or so, the books are still selling great. *Sex with Strangers* is the first one. No, it's not porn. It's not like porn porn. It started because I had this blog, but just a 'I'm nineteen and want to be a writer so read this' bullshit blog. But I wrote this kind-of funny story about this girl I met at a bar and how I ended up doing all this crazy shit to get her to have sex with me, but she wouldn't. My friends were like, yeah, girls won't fuck guys they just meet in bars anymore, because everyone meets online, pre-screens, you know? Even though half of what people say about themselves is bullshit. Anyway, I said in person still works if you can talk, most people just can't, or, not like I can. So, I bet my friends I could have sex with a stranger every week for a year. But the deal was, I had to go out to bars or wherever and meet girls the old-fashioned way, stranger to stranger. So, I started a blog about that. We call the book 'an internet memoir-based on the intoxicated recollections of a certifiable asshole'. I drink a lot. And, sometimes, I can't remember what the fuck happened. So, you know, I filled in some blanks, and maybe some things were exaggerated for the sake of a good story. But with that title, we covered our asses. The whole thing was actually much harder than I thought it'd be. But, finally, I ended up fucking this girl that had a really popular site and she linked to me when I wrote, in *awe*, about the fact that, in addition to being, like, crazy flexible, she could shoot, you know, shoot—out of her pussy! She could actually shoot her— Anyway, it was really funny. And after that I started getting a lot of hits and people got to know where I would hang out and then it was pretty easy since girls wanted to be written about in the blog. Some girl even started an 'I Fucked Ethan Strange' blog—she started the Ethan Strange thing. I was just plain Ethan Kane before that. And this online sort-of club was formed by girls who'd had sex with me. The site's still up.

Information on this playwright may be found at:
www.smithandkraus.com.
Click on the WRITERS tab.

Comic
Walt, thirty-eight

Walt Disney has Igor Stravinsky in his office, and is telling him what his animators on Fantasia are doing with "The Rite of Spring."

WALT: (He acts out as he describes.) Imagine if you will: your music starts—"Deeee dee-dee-dee-dee-deeee . . ."—and we open in the vast inky universe—below us, a swirling spiral galaxy; comets whiz by, stars burn in the cold vacuum of space. We truck into a single planet, red and shrouded, with a solitary moon. It's Earth, in its infancy, billions of years ago! All is barren and lifeless, except for the volcanoes, burbling with pools of lava. Here and there a small eruption, a boiling burp, and then suddenly, all hell breaks loose. The lava overruns the earth, moves boulders, reshapes mountains. The boiling rock hits the ancient ocean, and now great gusts of steam whip up, overwhelming the land, and the great elements of water and fire contend for supremacy. Earth, as we know it, is born. Soon we're in the primeval sea, and microscopic life takes hold:—then trilobites, hydras, eels, early fish—and one plucky fish in particular, we watch him as he slowly makes his way to land. It's the great leap of evolution! Jump a couple of million years, and now here come the dinosaurs. Brontosauruses feeding in the swamp, plesiosaurs, pterodactyls swooping down—you know that bit you have, what is it, a glissando? "buduluda-LING?"—and then we're in a swampy forest, with dimetrodons, triceratops . . . Those bastards have been stomping around in my brain for months. Parasaurolophuses, ornithomimuses...the slow-footed Stegosaurus, plodding along...The whole cast. All just going about their business, eating their plants, enjoying a very pleasant existence . . . And then the music changes, and the beasts look up from their meals—danger's approaching! The trees part, and suddenly there he is—Tyrannosaurus Rex, the King of the Dinosaurs! The other creatures, big and small, flee for their lives, but Stegy is caught. He rounds on the Tyrannosaurus, and the fight begins. Rex flashes his razor teeth. Stegy waves his spiky tail in reply. They clash! The battle is titanic, but it ends the only way it could have: poor Stegy, vanquished, dead. Tyrannosaurus roars triumphant, and feasts on his meal, as the other dinosaurs look on, frightened, envious. But even Rex has a limited reign, because now the sun beats down on a hard-baked earth, and the starving dinosaurs are scrabbling for food, poking through the mud, staggering on to the next water hole. We watch them walk off into the dust, the mist envelops them, and they're gone. Nothing remains but footsteps in the clay, fossils, bones. And then another cataclysm!—shattering earthquakes, tidal waves, once again the earth is covered with life-giving water, and it starts all over again. The Circle of Life. Fade out. Now how can you beat that?

Information on this playwright may be found at:
www.smithandkraus.com.
Click on the WRITERS tab.

Seriocomic
John, thirty-one

John is at a sex party. He's ducked into the kitchen for a cigarette, when in walks Julie, whom he hasn't met. He tells her s story about some goldfish he had to get for his employer, who is a photographer (and Julie's father).

JOHN: You know . . . you know, if you just call up a pet store, and ask for, like, three hundred goldfish or whatever, they don't want to sell them to you. Because they think you're using them for animal experiments, or something perverted, or whatever. I was like "Um, this is for a major American artist," and they were like "You're shitting us." Like, so much fucking attitude. So I got them online. It's like thirty dollars for a hundred. And then setting up the shot . . . Christ. So he has this photo now, okay, which is like three hundred goldfish in clear plastic baggies on a white carpet. It's kind of cool-looking. It's like you're looking down on these rows of goldfish. It looks great. It was a huge fucking pain in the ass. Well, once he's done, he doesn't want three hundred goldfish. He doesn't even want one in a bowl. So I had to call up the company and ask if I could ship back these goldfish—no, I'm serious. Because what can you do? And they were like, no, go fuck yourself. So then I called up the pet store—The *same* assholes that gave me all the attitude in the first place, and I was like, I want to sell you three hundred goldfish. And they were also like fuck you. But they would take them for free. And so now I have to get like three hundred goldfish to Union Square and your dad is like, great, so you can go do that now, and then he just like takes off. And I'm like, you asshole. You asshole, I'm expensing a cab. So I cabbed it with three hundred goldfish downtown and—are you an animal rights person? Because I gotta be honest with you, some of these goldfish did not survive the trip. *(Pause)* The rest are fine.

Information on this playwright may be found at:
www.smithandkraus.com. Click on the WRITERS tab.

Dramatic
John, thirty-one

John is at a sex party. He's experienced with these. Julie,
who he has just met when he ducked into the kitchen for a
cigarette, is not.

JOHN: I just think—I just think you should be careful, you
know, with what you say to people. Like—this is . . . this
is very much supposed to be a safe space. It's small, everybody knows everybody, everybody knows the rules, it's,
um . . . it's the kiddie pool, basically. But other places—I
don't know. People can get manipulative, sometimes
people can be, you know, disrespectful . . . It just . . . it
really depends on the culture. Like . . . I think everybody's
nice here. They're all my friends. But sometimes—I
mean, if you go to some of the bigger parties, the public
parties, the vibe is just . . . I'm trying to think of a good
way to put it . . . Just kind of domly . . . and sketchy . . .
I mean, not everybody is like this, not even all the het
dom guys at one party will be like this, but you'll have
guys who are just sort of there to cruise, basically, and
they see someone like you, and it's . . . it's fresh meat,
pretty much. I'm not . . . being too negative, or anything,
right? I just—my friend—this isn't really my story to
tell—Okay, well, there's this really big party they throw
in the Lower East Side once a month, they have this
huge venue, and they set up all this equipment for rope
suspensions. And they have a bar. So it's really popular.
And if you volunteer to come early and help set up the
equipment and get suspended so they can test everything
out, you can get in for free. I mean, if you're a girl and
you're cute and you volunteer, you can get in for free.
So that's what she did. And the guy who ran the whole

thing he was like, let's tie you up and suspend you and we can make sure the frame is set up okay. So she's tied up, and she's suspended from the frame they put up, and she can't move and he sticks his fingers into her and she can't move—And this is the guy who runs the thing, I mean he runs everything. And when he takes her down he was like, Whatever, I thought you were into it. And he just walks out. And, like . . . she didn't know what to do. And nobody wanted to talk about it. They were all like, I wasn't there, I don't know, I'm friends with the guy, he seems cool—I mean, nobody wanted to talk about it with her, you know? Like they were happy to say, oh, she's crazy, she's dramatic, but like . . . she got to the point where she was in so much pain, all the time, and nobody was like, okay maybe that guy is a dick. And I was like, I mean, I took her side, because of course, right, and people just wouldn't—like nobody would say to my face, you know, nobody would be like. "Hey John shut up about this already," but it felt that way all the time. I don't know. You know you get to choose what happens to you, right? I mean, there are guys, there are a ton of guys out there where you might play with them, like they might be good at something, but it's not going to be a sex thing. You do a scene, it's fun, you leave, that's it. That's how it is. If they want to fuck you they can ask but it's not your problem.

Information on this playwright may be found at:
www.smithandkraus.com. Click on the WRITERS tab.

Comic
Kyle, sixteen

*Kyle has written a play which he thinks is a sure-fire hit.
He is sending it off to "Broadway." This is his cover letter.*

KYLE: Dear Broadway. My name is Kyle Sugarman. It is
such a pleasure to meet you. I am currently a sophomore
at Harold Ferguson Senior High School just outside
Fort Collins, Colorado. Home of the Mighty Panthers.
I am an honors student. I have a three-six. I am also the
playwriter of my enclosed play which I am enclosing
here to send to you.
*(He reaches into a plastic bag and pulls out a thick script.
He smiles at the audience. He tosses the script onto the
floor where it lands with a BANG. The script should
be 350-502 pages.) He cocks his eyebrows as if to say,
"Impressive, huh?")*
My play is named Spacebar. I am basically positive that
you will find Spacebar to be the best play you've ever
read. Spacebar is a story about HUMANITY. I am 16 and
don't have an agent yet, but I ask that you please consider
Spacebar like it was written by some of my favorite play-
writers that do have incredible agents, like Neil Labute
or Shakespeare. My drama teacher, Mr. Ramirez, told
me that I should include a brief description of my play
in the cover letter which is what I'm about to do after
this colon:
(He pauses to indicate the colon.)
Let me clear something up right off the bat: Spacebar
is not about the space key on the computer keyboard.
Spacebar is about a bar in outer space. AND. It takes
place in the year nine-thousand-and-three. That's right,
Broadway, it's set in the FUTURE. You may be wonder-

ing how I, Kyle Sugarman, know what the world will be like in the year ninethousand-and—three. And the truth is: I don't. And this is definitely something Mr. Ramirez and I wrestled with. That's why I decided (and Mr. Ramirez agreed) that it would be a good idea to set Spacebar at a specific time in the Waaaaay Future. A time that will make this play completely produceable for the next roughly seven thousand years. And I am not bragging. Sophocles wrote 2,000 years ago and we're still doing his dumbass boring plays. You'll see that I attached my *business card*—

(He holds up a business card.)

Kyle Sugarman, Playwriter It has my personal home phone. If a woman answers, it's just my secretary. JK, Broadway. It's my Mom. So, yeah, take a look when you have a chance. Give it a little looksee. I'll just be here in Fort Collins, Colorado. Waiting. Sincerely and best, Kyle Sugarman PS—*Spacebar* is copyrighted so don't try any funny business!

Information on this playwright may be found at: www.smithandkraus.com. Click on the WRITERS tab.

Dramatic
Bogeyman, late thirties

When he was seven, David was raped by the teenaged son of friends of his parents, which emotionally scarred him for life. He has always thought of the boy who raped him as "The Bogeyman." Twenty years after he was raped, David has hatched a plan to kill the Bogeyman, who is now a father with kids of his own; but first he wants the Bogeyman to admit what he did

BOGEYMAN: I raped you, ok? I made you give me oral sex then I forced myself inside of you . . . I held a pillow over your head to cover the scr . . . *(He's doing everything he can to contain himself.)* I am so sorry David. I have no idea why I did that to you. I just acted on this one weird impulse. It's like it wasn't even me. It was sick and twisted and as soon as it was over, I was thinking, that's my friend . . . how could I have done that? Maybe it was an evil in me that I wasn't able to suppress, I don't know. Until I was in my 30's I didn't really believe that other people's feelings were real. I didn't think anyone really mattered but me. But I would do anything to undo what I did. I'll do anything now. Anything. I'll do anything you want me to do. I've thought a hundred times about contacting you in the last twenty years to tell you that . . . but I just never had the courage to pick up the phone. David, I don't know what else to say to you, but I'm begging you to forgive me. I know you have no reason to believe me, but I am a totally different person now. When I think back to who I used to be, it makes me sick. Maybe I don't deserve your forgiveness. But at least tell me that you are okay. I mean you look okay. You look healthy. I think my biggest fear was that I'd ruined your life. I was afraid that you would turn out to be a homeless drug addict or a drunk or something and it would all be my fault. Y'know having children changed my life. I found out what love really means. I used to think that love meant you just really liked somebody a whole lot. But when you become a father, you really understand what love is. David, I'll do anything you want me to do.

Information on this playwright may be found at: www.smithandkraus.com. Click on the WRITERS tab.

Dramatic
Bill, late twenties

Bill has recently been released from prison. A kid who works at Best Buy has stolen some expensive laptops, but he has gotten cold feat. Here. Bill reassures him that he has the situation well under control.

BILL: You asked me to move those Macbooks for you, you forgetting that? I didn't come into your store and pull you to the side and say, hey I see, ah, you know, I see a flaw in the way they're locking up those Macbook pros and why don't you plan on stealing a bunch of 'em and I can get rid of 'em for a good price, did I? No. Your buddy George told you about how I moved those air conditioners in two days, and you got to talking to me about how your boss, how, ah, Donald is such an idiot, leaves his keycard lying around, just asking someone to steal from 'em. Isn't that what you did? And all I said to you—the only thing I said to you was, well you let me know 'cause I can sure move a handful of Macbook computers, and even more'n a handful of Macbook computers, no problem. Ain't no one gonna look for 'em in my truck, good a hiding place as anywhere else. All right? And I'm done talking to you about this. You hear? There ain't no more to talk about. I'ma get these Macbook computers outta here as soon as goddamned possible. It ain't a problem. And now, you keep a damned lid on it til I do get 'em outta here. That's all you are gonna do, you ain't gonna talk to no one and you ain't gonna do nothing. And you ain't gonna come back to this place again. You hear me? Not ever. You ain't gonna drive by it on your way to somewhere else, you ain't gonna look it up on a map, you ain't even gonna think about this place right here or what I do or do not have in my truck parked there on the curb. Or I swear to

God, I will do everything I can to make sure you don't come out of this with just a slap on the damned wrist and the end of your days as a Best Buy bitch.

Information on this playwright may be found at:
www.smithandkraus.com. Click on the WRITERS tab.

Dramatic
Bill, late twenties

*Bill has recently been released from prison and is living with
his mother, who is a diabetic and is not allowed sweets. Bill
keeps finding hidden bags of candy. Julie, his ex-girlfriend
who now lives in Texas, has come over for a visit and she's
there while Bill lays into his Mom.*

BILL: I got secrets? You got secrets hidden all over the
goddamned house. I know you got all your little stashes
of something hidden around. Candy and sugar. Hiding
sweets and cookies and soda all around the house like a
goddamned junkie!
(to Julie)
Killing herself for some Oreo cookies or a Mars bar or
a cherry Coke—and I know it wasn't you bringing over
those chocolate kisses. She got those from some stockpile
she's keeping somewhere I ain't find it yet, but it ain't
my job—
(back to Sue)
—it ain't my job taking care of you twenty-four seven,
and maybe this woulda been Dad's job, but he ain't
here to do it and I swear to Christ, if this is what I got
stretching out ahead of me the next Lord knows how
many years, then I'm gonna get drowned in a river just
like he did and be done with the whole damn thing. So, I
tell you what, you want to put yourself into a sugar coma
or stroke or heart attack, or maybe you just want to eat
yourself to death, well you go ahead and do that and see
if that doesn't just make my life a hell of a lot easier.

*Information on this playwright may be found at:
www.smithandkraus.com. Click on the WRITERS tab.*

Dramatic
Nicholas, mid-twenties

*Having been visited by what he believes to be an alien
god who will soon whisk him away to the stars, Nicholas
argues about what punishment his roommate, Michael, and
Michael's girlfriend Ianthe, deserve for trying to sneak off
without him.*

NICHOLAS: You're no good, Mike. You're no good at all.
And you're a liar and you're not even good at that. I
don't know how you found out about it, but it's not for
you. We're gonna have a trial, huh? I've always thought
. . . have you ever read Hobbes? *The Leviathan?* No? Of
course not. Ianthe, you've read Thomas Hobbes, right?
See! There's another thing! Don't let me get off track.
Hobbes got me thinking a lot about capital punishment, if
it's moral or not, you see. And I'm not sure if it serves a
greater good, but that really isn't the issue, the way I see
Hobbes. It's more about the terms of the contract—social
contract. The thing is, in Hobbes day, death wasn't—being sentenced to death, I mean—wasn't the worst punishment. Banishment. You know, exile? Even up when
Shakespeare wrote, right Ianthe? Juliet says something
about banishment being worse than death? Anyway, so
morally, I think we've got the right to it—execution,
not exile, we can obviously morally exile people even
though we don't anymore, so maybe not—I think, except
for some little problems, and one of those is innocence.
If someone is innocent but convicted, and we kill the,
well, then, no one is safe. I'm not sure a state can ever
know, I mean really know that a person is guilty, know
well enough to kill them. But I can. I can know that.
About the two of you. And don't worry! We're talking
about something safer here. But worse, I think. Like in

Hobbes' day. Not even entering the suicide element. And I think I know . . . goes without saying, right? But I'm willing to entertain arguments. Willing to hear the story.

Dramatic
Tycho, late forties to early fifties

Near death, the pioneering astronomer Tycho Brahe contemplates his wasted years to his apprentice, Johannes Kepler, who may very have killed him.

TYCHO: When I was young and I looked at the stars, I saw magic. "What are these things?" I would wonder. And the planets! The planets, which then seemed different from stars just barely, just the difference in color and magnitude. But as I grew and watched I saw them move. Saw the planets move in a way that the stars did not. That was a slow epiphany . . . that things which seem so similar, marvelous things, could actually be entirely different. I followed Mars so intently. Years. Every night I would mark it, observe it. And then, finally, when I had it all down, I started on Venus . . . didn't even take a moment to breathe. But in the middle of my studies, I thought I had it figured out. Thought I could predict the whole thing. I looked up from my abacus and realized I could chart the rest without even looking. Just for a moment, that's what I thought. I dropped my guard. I had gone about my work with teeth-grating enthusiasm and intensity. So long as I kept up my drive, it seemed like I could go forever. But that one hesitation, that one lag . . . doomed me. I didn't know it at first, you see, but it did, it doomed me. I'm convinced. From there is all fizzled, like the weight of my scales had just flipped. It became more about what I had, and what I had done than what I might do. Gladly. I had lived well, and it was time to celebrate that. You see? It was the celebration: it just swallowed me whole.

Dramatic
Malcolm, mid-twenties

Malcolm has never strayed far from his mother because his father left them when Malcolm was young and his mother took it hard. After dinner with his mother on a snowy evening, Malcolm hears her breathe shallowly from upstairs. Has something happened? Instead of seeing the truth (she has suffered a stroke), he comforts himself with a story of the two of them on an adventure in a flooded world.

MALCOM: The bed hits the door frame head-on. But it's too big to fit through the door. I hear this big rush of water. I crawl to the end of the bed and I see it. The stairs. Water's rushing down the stairs, creating a fall, like some kind of log flume. I hear another rush. The window on the left's broken open, water comes pouring in, creating a wave that pushes the bed sideways, spinning it around. Mom, Hold On! And the force has moved the bed sideways. And another wave pushes the bed again, dislodging it past the doorframe. And now we are heading full-speed towards the stairs. Oh shoot shoot. And down we go. Fast. The bed is cast down the stairs by the water. For a moment, I feel the bed go airborne, above the torrent of water propelling down the stairs, and we hit the wall at the the the landing. We hit the wall and no longer airborne, the tide pushes us down the remaining stairs even faster. Water's hitting my face, but still the bed's floating, we aren't taking on that much water. And then in front of me, the front door. Except the door's gone. Been cracked by the force of the water. And the current from the falls that were once the stairs of my parent's house pushes the floating bed with me and my mother out in into the morning air, out into the front yard, which is no longer a front yard, but a vast ocean where nothing's visible except submerged trees and in the distance, the submerged houses of the neighbors. And we are traveling. Me and my mom. And I turn and I see this, this, this, um, this sight, this this wall of water that's forming behind my parent's home and hear the terrible crack a caterwauling sound of the sheer massive density of water bursting over and through and under this house forming a tidal wave the likes of which I've never seen and most likely the likes of which I will never see again because a human try as he might cannot help but be awed by the impressive sight of nature unfurled even if he knows that this sight this massive body of water speeding towards him might in fact be the final sight he will ever see.

Information on this playwright may be found at:
www.smithandkraus.com.
Click on the WRITERS tab.

Dramatic
Walter, sixty-six

Elliott, a sometime actor, has written a play and has asked Walter, who was married to his deceased sister, what he thinks of it. Walter has told him that he thinks it's appallingly bad, and then lays into Elliott, telling him why his acting career never went anywhere.

WALTER: You think coming in to audition is hard? Try sitting on the other side of the table for a change. Actors I've known for thirty, forty years—people I started out with, people I admired—schlep in to read. Angry. Desperate. Cracking too many jokes, laughing too hard. Pushing it. You smell flop sweat the way a dog smells fear. It's awful seeing people you care about so exposed, just horrible. I've sat there when you›ve come in, Elliot. Failure and aggression follow you into the room. Like a storm cloud. With this Fuck-you, I-don't-need-you chip on your shoulder. The vibe you give off . . .You don't want the job. You think you should want it; you go through the motions. But you don't. Not really. Because if you got the job you'd have to deliver, and you're terrified that you won't be able to do it. You'd bomb out. Or, worse, you couldn't cut it and I'd have to fire you. *(A beat.)* No one wants to work with you, Elliot. You've done a very good job of making yourself radioactive. You're on everyone's life-is-too-short list.

Information on this playwright may be found at:
www.smithandkraus.com.Click on the WRITERS tab.

Dramatic
Walter, sixty-six

Walter is a successful film director who was married to Elliott's lately-deceased sister. Elliott, a failed actor, has accused Walter, a once highly-regarded stage director, of selling out by doing films which appeal to moronic 15 year-olds. Walter responds.

WALTER: Grow up, Elliot. Selling-out is a young person's idea. An adolescent's romantic notion that in order to be an artist you need to starve and suffer; commercial success is the devil's work. Well, I say, nuts to that. I was the paragon of nothing. I was a pragmatist who got sick of filling my calendar just to make enough to scrape by, and wanted to make some real money for a change! If you think I've lost any sleep over this . . . I have nothing against 15-year-old boys; they're as legitimate a demographic as any. 15-year-old boys have made me rich. I am indebted to them. Call it pandering if you like. I call it commerce. I provide a product to a vastly appreciative audience. I made this choice, long ago, no looking back, no regrets. What should I regret? The work on stage I didn't do? Not a chance. Starvation is not a virtue. I've tried it. It takes just as much energy and imagination making good, commercial entertainment than it does to make so-called art. So why not get paid for it? I discovered there will always be 15-year-old boys, an endless supply, ad infinitum, who go to the movies to watch all the cool different ways you can blow stuff up. I happen to like that, too. The thea-tuh, the thea-tuh. If I hear one more time how I abandoned the fucking thea-tuh. . . The grandiosity of theater people! Who have convinced themselves that what they do is of a higher order than all other forms of make believe! What an odd pursuit, when you stop to think about it: Grown people shouting in rooms missing a fourth wall?

Information on this playwright may be found at:
www.smithandkraus.com.
Click on the WRITERS tab.

Dramatic
Elliott, mid to late forties

Elliott's mother is a theatre and film star. He has written a play, which his family thinks is terrible, which so upset him that he went running off. He has returned from wandering around in the woods and tells Michael, a TV star who is staying at his mother's house in Williamstown while he does a play, that he has had an epiphany.

ELLIOT: I had an epiphany. My mother doesn't love me. You think all women love their children? Medea? Gertrude? Not all women should be mothers. It wasn't a role that came naturally to her. She was miscast. And spent all these years "indicating" like crazy: the least convincing performance of her career. *(A beat)* Did you know I had a stutter? I did. *(whispers)* Something we don't talk about. *(normal volume)* I'm a recovering stutterer. Like being an alcoholic: you're never really cured. Always one consonant, one breath away from an avalanche. Whenever I spoke, I'd see Mother, clenched jaw, frozen smile, staring into her salad, or down at her shoes, and imagine her thinking, like a thought-bubble in a comic book: "Get on with it, Elliot, for God's sake, don't humiliate yourself, or more importantly, me." And I'd get so nervous, I'd lose traction and fly off the rails. She set me up! Over and over again! She wanted me to fail! She does it to this day! Whenever I open my mouth! *(A beat)* Listen to me: What a joke I am, huh? *(mock tears)* "My mother doesn't love me."

Information on this playwright may be found at:
www.smithandkraus.com.
Click on the WRITERS tab.

Dramatic
Elliott, mid to late forties

Elliott and his family have gathered together at his mother's country house to mourn the one year anniversary of the death of his sister, a successful actress. Elliott's mother is a stage and film star. Elliott has been a failure at acting and playwriting. Here, he tells his family that he wishes he had died instead of his sister.

ELLIOT: Mother. I so wish it had been me. I should have been the one who died. An early death would have lent my life a little dignity, y'know? A touch of tragedy. It would have been so much better all around. Oh, come on, don't pretend you haven't thought it. *(Pause)* Look at me, Mama: How did this happen to me? How did I become this . . . sad excuse for a man? I wasted so much time! On what? Auditions! Rehearsals for living, not living. Kathy dies. My magnificent sister. Of lung cancer! Never smoked a day in her life. And I, with my self-destructive habits and . . . mediocrity, get to go on breathing? Why? It doesn't make sense. I don't interest you. Do I? Do I interest you. Answer the question. You could at least make a show of protest. All my life . . . I've been the only nobody in the room. I have dropped your name to people I wanted to like me. Directors have cast me in plays hoping you'd show up opening night—which of course, you never did. I had promise. Once. *(a la Brando)* "I coulda been a contenda. I coulda been somebody." Comedy! I did improv at school. But you never came to see me! You were always working. I was good! I was funny! If only you had seen for yourself! But, no, you didn't come. You assumed I'd be bad. Kathy you saw in every damn thing she was in. If she was one of a multitude of sugarplum fairies, you were there! Would it have taken so much to offer me even the slightest bit of encouragement? Would it? You were so . . . withholding, so stingy, as if offering praise meant giving up a vital part of yourself. If only you had told me I was good at something! Instead you told me I was hopeless, there was nothing I did well. How could you deprive your child of hope?! It's unnatural. Y'know? When I was a boy . . . and you'd go off to the theater? I'd wait up for you to come home, force myself to stay awake 'till one or two in the morning. My heart would pound when I'd hear your keys jingle and your footsteps in the hall, and pray you'd come in to kiss me. You'd breeze in, in the dark, smelling like night, cold cream on your cheek. I'd lay there pretending to be asleep because I knew that if you found out I waited up, you would stop coming in and that would be that. I spent years at grade school exhausted from lack of sleep—until one night you discovered my gambit, and those goodnight kisses came to an end. I'm still that boy in the dark, praying for your kiss.

Information on this playwright may be found at:
www.smithandkraus.com.
Click on the WRITERS tab.

Dramatic
Tom, thirties

*Allie's husband; a gregarious, natural salesman Tom is
already late to an important meeting with his wife, Allie,
and Claire, the Director of Parent Services at a donor
insemination research program for 'exceptional' children.
The program not only provided the 'genius' sperm for
their son Michael but has paid for his prestigious private
school and other expensive services that Allie and Tom
could never have afforded since Michael was born. Tom,
currently unemployed, has just come from an important job
interview, and Allie, who feels they will need his income to
make having a second child feasible, is anxiously awaiting
the outcome. Having already turned it down, Tom enters,
nervous but hopeful that he can somehow convince Allie to
agree with his decision.*

TOM: Well, not exactly . . . I was let go, but Joe's a pretty
astute reader of men, and he said my nonverbals were
coming through loud and clear. Of course it doesn't
take long to start missing the paycheck, so when this
headhunter called about Murphy and Finn . . . better
product line, big hike in pay . . . of course I've done my
homework, I know exactly what this guy needs, so I
start right in, and he's loving it. I'm only penciled in for
30 minutes, but it's been 50, and I'm still on a roll, when
halfway through a sentence I stop, because it's suddenly
clear . . . so I tell him, "Look, Murph" . . . that's what he
asked me to call him . . . 'Murph' . . . "I could do this job
in my sleep and still make you money, but hearing myself aloud, I know that coming on board at this juncture
would be a colossal mistake. If I don't take stock of my
life and figure out what I really want, I probably never
will." So Murph leans back and starts telling me how

after his wife divorced him, he drank a fifth of scotch a day, ignored his personal hygiene and started keeping a loaded gun in his desk, until his sponsor made him take a personal inventory, which looking back was the single most important thing he ever did. *(Beat. Disconcerted by the lack of reaction, he is at a loss but then throws himself into his other argument.)* And truthfully, I'm not terribly sanguine about where the calibration industry is heading in this country. Don't be surprised if you wake up one morning, and the entire concept has been shipped overseas. But if you want to think 'big picture' . . . for every guy who's standing there with a pink slip saying life isn't fair . . . that's maybe four guys in Mexico who finally have a job . . . you know what I mean?

Dramatic
Bryan, late thirties-early forties

Bryan and his girlfriend QZ started a small newspaper to serve long-haul truckers and made their trailer park home into a kind of haven for them. Bryan has returned after disappearing for four years to find that a troubled teen named Matthew is living there and helping QZ put out the paper. Here, he tells him about why that started it.

BRYAN: Look, when we started this thing, it . . . *(pause)* Jim and I started trucking around the same time, thought the money would be good. Plus QZ and I were fighting all the time, thought'd be good for us to get some distance. For a while, it was, but . . . *(pause)* It does something to you, driving that much. Jim and I were doing runs across the whole country, easily saw forty-eight states between the two of us. After a while—you start to feel like you don't exist. Like you're never in a place long enough to even exist. You stop talking to people at gas stations and truck stops, you start avoiding the restaurants where the waitresses might recognize you, you start sleeping in the back of your cab just so you don't have to talk to a motel clerk. You go to diners and truck stops full of other long-haul guys, and you don't even look at each other. *(pause)* One night, Jim and I were both doing runs. I was in Utah, he was in North Carolina or something. He gives me a call, and he says he's at a truck stop—he says that he can't see anyone's faces. He says he's looking at people's faces, trying to see them—but he can't see anything. *(pause)* That night, I guess—I decided to do something. I quit trucking, sunk the inheritance from my dad into this place. We just thought it could be a place where truckers could just—look at each other, talk. Remind each other that they still existed. Jim called it "church without God." And it was. Pretty soon, long-haul guys were stopping by almost every night, just to talk. A lot of the time it was just daily stuff—long-distance marriages, gas prices, that kind of stuff. But every so often there'd be some guy, some trucker from some random corner of some random state who was amazing, come in and tell us a story about driving a tanker in the middle of a hurricane, or show us pictures he'd taken of sunrises at McDonald's in forty-three different states. And after a while, Jim and I decided to just—write it down.

Information on this playwright may be found at:
www.smithandkraus.com.
Click on the WRITERS tab.

Comic
Dodd, late thirties to fifties

*Dodd has tricked Victoria, his ex-girlfriend, into joining him
in the suburbs of eastern Long Island where he is directing
a play in a man's garage. He told her he was directing a
workshop at a "major regional theatre." The two had not
spoken in months, since Dodd cheated on her during their
outdoor Shakespeare production the previous summer. She
has just arrived, and has demanded the truth about this play.*

DODD: "What am I doing?" quoth you! Well! You, and I,
are, first, being paid to work on a play. To develop, to
workshop a new, original, American theatre piece. You
are a serious committed actress who is now employed.
At work. Second, we are in no man's land on eastern
Long Island, staying in bedrooms right next door to each
other. So we are also at play. You're saving me Vicky.
How could I do this gig by myself? I've been out here
for three days. Doing what it is I do! Working with a cast
of actors, and a playwright. I don't know him! I never
met him before in my life. Bob Malone. He's some guy
who saw the play last summer. He found my website
and called me. And pitched me. Hired me to stage his
play. Here. In his garage on Long Island. Holding back
laughter, and a yawp of horror, I told him what I'd re-
quire, including 'my usual union rate,' which I invented
on the spot, and he agreed! Vicky, this guy's a huge find!
He owns his own landscaping company. Cleverly titled,
Malone Landscaping Company. I need a donation for
the company. I want to do Cymbeline next summer, but
this time up on the field near 103rd Street, and I want to
hire a publicist—get some important people in the audience—not just these ignorant gapers who have no idea
what they're witnessing. You're getting a hundred sixty

a day! When's the last time you could say that! When have you ever said that? And look at this. He made us a little black box! Smells like tires, but you get used to it. And how am I taking advantage? A man is writing for the stage and I'm commissioned to help, to elevate his work, teach him something about the theatre. He's got their whole family coming, apparently. One performance. That's it, then we all go home. *(a beat)* The play is, not really a play. It's him and his wife. Their courtship, years ago. In verse. A syllabic, half-Alexandrine, Sesame Street verse. You'll be great. Oh come on! I need you! Right now the cast is his deaf father-in-law and a couple townies. The girl playing the wife couldn't stop laughing in rehearsal. That gave me my excuse to call you in. She's now taking over my ensemble roles so I can just focus on directing. Now you're playing the young wife. Pretend it's some rural, artsy . . . pretend it's the O'Neill Conference. Everyone involved is boarding here at his house. Your room is the little yellow one next to mine. *(pause)* Hey it beats on-camera acting class, doesn't it? Beats the restaurant, doesn't it? Any other important business you'd be missing next couple days?

Information on this playwright may be found at:
www.smithandkraus.com.
Click on the WRITERS tab.

THE HUNCHBACK OF SEVILLE
Charise Castro Smith

Comic
Christopher Columbus, forty-one (but could be
played by an actor of any age)

Columbus has just landed in the new world and here addresses his crew and the audience.

CHRISTOPHER COLUMBUS: My name is Christopher
Columbus and I claim this whole entire land-place that
you all people see here before you and which we can
legally term "The West Indies." Since we obviously
did our goal and got to India in the name of Spain and
all its subsequent domicilios, provinces and corporations. These are the true feelings I carried within my
heart-breast on this most momentous moment in world
universal history: My name is Cristoforo Colombo and
I claim this whole entire land-place (which I will call it
this in my mind only because my benefactors are papists
and look disagreeably on foul languages, okay. And also
because I was supposed to be locating India but instead
I happened to make us come to) THE NEW FUCKING
WORLD in the name of me me me Cristoforo Colombo!!
And I hereby wish my máma was here to see this because
she would be really proud of me and also let it hereby
be known that although the repercussions and enormity
of this discovery are yet unbeknownst to my conscious
mind, deep in the eaves of my brain I know, oh bambino
do I ever know that I have found something here on these
virginish shores which will prove even more alluring
than, indeed, all the perfumes and spices of Araby. And
to every small person in Genoa who looked at me and
said: 'Ooooh! Cristoforo Colombo is a poopy little kid
who works at his daddy's cheese stand and is largely
self-educated and misinterpreted much of what he read

as modern historians have pointed out from the notes he made in the margins of his copy of 'The Travels of Marco Polo' and also he poops his pants!' And to everybody back in Europe who dares to think in private or utter in public: 'I think privately and say publicly that there is a compelling body of evidence that Christopher Columbus did not actually reach India like he said he did because according to widely accepted calculations of how big the actual earth is, there is no way that a boat during our times could go so fast that it would reach India without them running out of provisions and starving to death...' And to everybody in the modern days whose like: 'You are a backwards imperialist douchebag with an overinflated ego and also you are responsible largely for one of history's most horrible genocides' I say: 'Do YOU have a holiday named after you in the United States of America 505 years after your death?' Okay, so guess who is famous and guess who is not.

Information on this playwright may be found at:
www.smithandkraus.com.
Click on the WRITERS tab.

Seriocomic
Talib Furozh, thirties

*Talib is an algebra tutor and banished Moor in 1504. He's
talking to his lover (an agoraphobic Hunchback, and Queen
Isabella's secret twin sister). The dramatic context is that
he's just returned Spain from his exile in the New World
and is struggling to come to terms with the atrocities of
the inquisition.*

TALIB FUROZH: Maxima baby, I'm so tired that I just want
to die. It's like, we roll into the world as these happy fat
little gods right? And if we've got any sort of luck our
mothers love us and teach us for years that the world is
not such a bad place- sure there's stuff we're not supposed
to touch cause we'll get burnt or something but mostly
if we can keep our bodies safe then we'll be okay and
afterwards we might even get a toy and go to sleep and
dream . . . But then as you grow up your start to realize
that It's not just keeping your hands away from flames but
that there are people out there that want to kill you just
because you are a Moor and the Queen of Spain decides
that you and all your people need to leave right away. Or
because you were an entire civilization of people living
separate lives an ocean away from Spain and then one
day a bunch of cockholes on boats literally descend
upon you and not only infect everyone with foreign
diseases but also torture and kill everybody and then
also kill your soul by telling you that you deserve it
because God hates who you are. And you can come
back home and hide away and be temporarily isolated
from the completely random utter brutality of the
world. I was there Maxima. None of that matters. I saw
what those people did, And I can never not know it. I
give up. I just can't believe that I was born at such a

relentlessly shitty point in history and there's nothing I can do about it.

Information on this playwright may be found at:
www.smithandkraus.com.
Click on the WRITERS tab..

Seriocomic
Steve, forty-eight

Steve is an action movie star, and not exactly the bright-est bulb in the pack. He and his much younger wife Missy have been invited to dinner by Karen, his co-star in his next movie. Karen's girlfriend Bev is highly antagonistic towards him, principally because she thinks he's an ignorant lout. She has accused him of fathering several illegitimate children. He tells her there are only two.

STEVE: God, don't make it sound like I'm running around just . . . I've done the blood tests on those two and all that shit and they're definitely mine but I had to fight a couple cases in court. Cover of *US Weekly* three weeks running!! Yeah, I bet you've seen a few mentions of it out there . . . *Entertainment Tonight* was camped on my fucking doorstep for a month at one point! Seriously. Got to a place where I was taking bagels and coffee out to them in the morning! Yep. I'd open my door to get the paper—I'm someone who actually enjoys reading the *L.A. Times*, it's got very good sports coverage and the Calendar section's been very nice to me, not just Kenny Turan but several of their——anyway, I literally had Mary Hart at the end of the driveway. . . handing me the early edition, six in the morning! Lady is very sweet—she's got beautiful legs on 'er—but shit . . . come on! That's crazy! Even by, like, movie star standards, that's crazy!! I am not Cher, my kid didn't chop his dick off and become a chick or something like that so what is up? Right?! *(Beat)* This town's insane, honestly . . . you move here and you go bonkers in two, three years, tops. I mean it. It's like a big asylum plopped down near the ocean...the weather's great, you make a lotta money . . . but we are all fucking nuts and it's everybody, down to the last man.

That's why nobody realizes it . . . you don't even know it 'cause you're living right in the middle of it! Anyhow, yeah, I got two kids. A boy and a girl. *(Beat)* I probably don't see 'em enough or spend as many holidays as I'd like to . . . I want to, I do . . . something always seems to come up, though. *(Beat)* But yeah . . . we hope to have a baby . . . Missy and me. Of our own.

Dramatic
Dante, early forties

Dante is reconnecting with three buddies at his 25th high school reunion. Here, he talks about what their friendship means to him.

DANTE: I'm gonna tell you an anecdote. *(clears throat . . .)* I remember a day in college when you and Reg came and visited me. Freshman year in college, when we were all still sorta homesick for high school. And it was a beautiful fall day and we were lying out on this field. And we were out there smoking pot and drinking beer and taking 'shrooms and dropping acid. Listening to Beatles songs in a whole new way. And we were discussing the nature of friendship. I remember having just been introduced to Mr. Martin Buber—me, the little Catholic boy swimming gloriously in the sea of Jewish mysticism for the very first time . . . And what I remember most from the conversation is actually you, Les, and your response to the whole topic. At first you were quiet as hell, but after a while you spoke up. Do you remember what you said? What you said was, "Dante, none of us here, at this point in life, can come close to defining friendship, much less truly living it. But this much I can guess at: Friendship is a form of Godliness. It is our way into the divine. It is our core. And when we're there, we'll know because our sense of loyalty will run deep like a river and our call to action, when the shit hits the fan, will hurtle us forward with every particle of our body, from the tips of our brain to the muscles in our toes."

Information on this playwright may be found at:
www.smithandkraus.com.
Click on the WRITERS tab.

Seriocomic
Jim, early forties, African-American

Jim, who owns a sneaker company, has been missing in Chad for three months, presumed to have been kidnapped by terrorists. Then he shows up at his 25th high school re-union, where he tells four of his male classmates, who have been trying to come up with a plan to rescue him, what he in fact was doing those three months.

JIM: As you guys probably read about in last May's profile of me in *Sneaker Monthly*, I was *whoppingly* successful: I had money, I was a sneaker supernova, I'd gone bowl-ing *more than once* with Drake . . . but I still wasn't the man I'd always aspired to be. And it hit me when I was over there, like a smack from God's hammer. The day I throttled a goat and ate its balls. Glancing around at my factory workers, people making *60 cents* an hour, I said to myself: This is *not* the embodiment of the dreams I used to have. Plus I met Suli-SanSillo. Hot as fuck. But the *point* is, I want my life to be about more. More *activism*. More sweaty intensity. I'm here to spread the word, Les, to stand up for the values of my Chiakka-Suni brothers and of my brothers' brothers' *brothers* throughout this country. To use but not abuse the power given to me by the Sneaker gods above, to spread the wealth and maintain the health, to enliven and agitate, to ministrate and navigate the complexities of this country so that all men—and all the lady-folks as well—so that we are all given a fair goddam shake of the Koomi-Sani rattle! (and then) And now, to see you guys up here; my boys, my *brothers from other mothers*; my high school homies, my catchers in the rye—the men that I was *formed* with!—seeing you right now makes me cry a little. On the inside. *(and then, with fondness)* I love you men. Back in the day we were like a fist—the five of us? Like a tightly compacted fist, fully clenched, probing for something real, a fist inside the system, inside the asshole of the system, working our way toward truth, no matter the blood and guts.

Information on this playwright may be found at:
www.smithandkraus.com.
Click on the WRITERS tab.

Dramatic
Donell, twenty, African-American

Donell is fighting Jas Dennis tonight. If he beats him, it will be a huge boost for his prizefighting career. Here, he's talking with his trainer, Tre, during a workout.

DONELL: My goal's to win the fight. I win the fight and then later when he sees what I got then he thinks, "I had that car and that house and look what Donell Fuseles's got—he's got more than what I coulda thought, he saw higher than I did." That shit's gonna burn him, gonna burn anybody lookin' to fight me, everybody noticing how much I got, when I drive up to the fight in my new car, when I come into the building with my group—trainer, manager, crew, alla them—when I come into the ring with all of the people surrounding me, with my robe just right, my shoes looking good, from in the ring to out, I'm lookin' like they never could, they see me and say, "That guy beat so many fighters that he's got all that shit. What fuckin' chance I got to beat him since he's got everything like that, there's no way to win." He's got the dream and I want to distort that dream by making it my dream, but expanded. I'll get what he has but I'll get better and then he'll see I ain't messin' around. Jas thinks he's got it good, that house and that car, and I want to show him I'm gonna get better. That's all there is to what I'm sayin'. That he'll see when it's over what the truth of the matter is. That I'm the goddamn best there is. *(beat)* Right this minute, Jas Dennis wondering who I am. Who the hell is this guy. Right now, Jas Dennis is worryin' I could take his dreams.

Dramatic

Robbie, seventeen

Robbie is the son of Dr. and Mrs. Sidney Rosenstein of Ditmas Park, Brooklyn; the year is 1956. He is responding to the audience question, "Rebel without a cause?"

ROBBIE: You calling me a rebel? Just 'cause I play the guitar? 'Cause I like to rock and roll? Go ahead. Call me a rebel. I hang with the cool cats. Might join a gang. Plenty of gangs in Brooklyn. Hey doll face, you think I'm a rebel? Maybe I am. Soon as I can, I'm packing up my 45s and my guitar and I am getting out of Brooklyn. Nothing going on here. See, I like to rock and roll and drive a car low to the ground. Like to cut school, too. I'm too cool for school. I'm thinking of dropping out. Might as well. Not like I'm gonna be a doctor or a dentist. I gotta get out of here bad. Wanna drive to California, where the girls are different. Where the music makes them melt. Ditmas Park? Too small for me. Everybody knows everybody. I've had enough of these busy bodies. Gonna drive until I reach that sign in the hills: "Hollywood." I'll go in for one of those screen tests. Make a film or two. Like James Dean. Better than playing stick ball on the streets of Brooklyn. In my dreams, I'm flying through the sky, over all the bodegas in Brooklyn, waving bye-bye to the goody-two shoe girls who are stuck in their rooms . . . Scram now. I said scram!

Dramatic
Ellis, early forties

Ellis is talking to his daughter, Catherine, whom he hasn't seen since she was 9 months old. Ellis is bipolar with psychosis. During a psychotic episode, he killed a little boy, thinking he was an ocelot.

ELLIS: Sometimes when I close my eyes there are cats and ocelots and burning trees. And sometimes the trees run like men on fire and sometimes there are ocelots up in the branches and they're burning too. And there's this hole in the ground that's actually a giant lion's mouth with fangs and sometimes horses come riding up out of it and they're on fire too, like hundreds of them and they're coming for me and there's nowhere for me to be, and the floor falls away, and all the doors start boiling, and bats, too, thousands of them peppering the sky, and and and *sometimes* . . . sometimes when this happens, when I'm overwhelmed by these images, I picture you . . . like what I thought you would wind up looking like, which is pretty similar to what you look like right now, except in my head maybe you're a little taller and you have my nose, not your mother's, which is definitely a better nose, meaning your mother's nose is better . . . and you're flying that kite I gave you, the red one in the box, that's why I bought it in the first place, because I always see you flying it . . . And for whatever reason, when I picture this, it makes all the other stuff go away. The cats and the ocelots and the burning trees and the giant lion's mouth hole and the horses on fire and the thousands of bats peppering the sky . . . And then it's just you flying your kite . . . Like in a field with long grass . . . Just you with your red kite . . . And it's good, Catherine . . . It makes all that stuff go away and, well, I feel better . . . I wanted to tell you that because that's the truth. Sometimes the medication isn't as effective as it can be and I have a bad day and I can't seem to make sense of what's in my refrigerator or I wake up on my bathroom floor when I fell asleep in my bed, or it feels like my left hand has fallen off and I can't seem to find it anywhere . . . Catherine, I left you and your mother because I was afraid I was going to hurt you. I'm so sorry . . . .

THE ROAD TO DAMASCUS

Tom Dulack

Dramatic
Dexter Hobhouse, fifties

*Dexter, a State Dept. official, has gone to the Vatican to try
and persuade the Pope not to fly to Damascus just before
the U.S. bombs it into rubble in retaliation for a terrorist
bombing in New York which the U.S. government believes
was masterminded by Syria. A Vatican official has shown
him intel which shows that, in fact, the Syrians had nothing
to do with it—and the U.S. knows it. Dexter has resigned
and gone "off the grid." Here, he is speating to Nadia, a
reporter for PanArabya television and his lover.*

HOBHOUSE: I resigned because I saw some things, some
    classified documents, that made it impossible for me to
    continue working for the government. It's Qatar that's
    funding the Army of God. The attacks on both Miami
    and New York were funded directly by the ruling families
    in Qatar. Dubai and The Emirates are also implicated.
    Damascus didn't have anything to do with the attacks.
    Nothing. And Washington knows this. I've seen cables,
    I've read intercepted emails, transcripts of phone calls.
    Washington knows. The State Department knows. Qatar
    and the Emirates are afraid that they are the next logical
    target of the Army of God. So it behooves them to keep
    the US and the militants at each other's throats. Think
    about it. All those Oxford educated sheikhs driving
    around in their Jaguars, and flying their private jets, and
    cruising in their palatial yachts. Launching film festivals
    and beauty contests. You've heard of the Race to Dubai?
    A year-long pilgrimage with professional golfers compet-
    ing for millions of euros is not exactly the pilgrimage to
    Mecca. That's the real new face of Islam. And they're
    scared to death of a Caliphate in Syria. A Caliphate in
    Syria is their worst nightmare. So they keep dangling

the bait and we keep swallowing it without realizing that eventually this Frankenstein monster that we have unwittingly conspired to create will kill us all. The evidence is overwhelming. And State knows it, the Pentagon knows it. But they continue to blame Damascus and we're going in putting boots on the ground yet again, and we will be enmeshed in yet another Middle Eastern war for the next ten years and it will finish us as a nation once and for all.

Dramatic
Augustine, fifties to sixties, African

Augustine, the first African Pope, plans to fly to Damascus in hopes that his presence there will deter the U.S. from bombing it into rubble in retaliation for a terrorist bombing in New York, which the Americans think Syria masterminded. He is talking to his Secretary of State, who has been trying to persuade him not to go. Here, he tells him why he must go.

AUGUSTINE: The Muslim is our brother, Fernando. And there is no one else to defend him from America's bombs. We have the same truth, Islam and the Church. And the truth is light, and people all over the world struggle towards this light. The struggle is what counts, the light is what counts. It is what they believe and it is what I believe. I cannot believe that the Holy Spirit approves of my sitting idly by while human life on this planet comes to a fiery end. I don't know why you all elected me to be your pontiff. I didn't want it, I don't deserve it. Nevertheless, you chose me three months ago. And now I'm here. And there must be a reason God wanted me here. And I believe that it was for me to stop this war. In Cordoba, there is a cathedral lodged in the middle of the one of the most famous and beautiful mosques ever built. And in Istanbul, after the Muslims recaptured the city in 1453, they did not destroy Saint Sophia as they might have been expected to do. They built a mosque inside the church. We cannot release each other, Islam and Catholicism. We cannot disengage from each other. We are locked in a perpetual embrace and will be locked in this embrace until the end of time. An attack on Damascus is the same as an attack on Rome. It is not heresy. But, if it takes a heresy to prevent the extinction of human life on this planet, so be it. I'm not speaking in abstractions or in metaphors! I'm speaking about innocent men and women and children being incinerated in their beds, in their schools, while they are at work, at their prayers. Innocent people, Fernando. Innocent souls.

Eric Coble

Dramatic
Chris, late forties

*Chris has been asked by his siblings to try and persuade
their mother to leave her house and go into a home. She
refuses and is threatening to blow up the house, and herself.*

CHRIS: You want to know why I stay away, it's 'cause I
know coming to this house is gonna be like visiting the
witches in Macbeth! Here's my own ghastly nightmare
future staring back at me from your crazy eyes—"Behold
what you will become, Christopher Benton, here is your
old age and it is ugly as hell!" You're threatening to burn
down our house, Mom! You've got a son and daughter
outside wetting themselves over whether or not to warn
the neighbors about their pyro mother! They gave me an
hour, Mom—One Hour—before they call the cops, and
then there is no going back. You are locked up or you are
dead if that happens. That's tear gas, that's SWAT teams,
that's snipers on the roof across the street to shoot you in
the head! That's why they called me! That's why I flew
in here middle of the goddam night because Michael
and Jen knew you wouldn't talk to them and maybe, just
maybe, I could somehow talk sense into your deranged
thick-headed skull and I—stupid, foolish, idiot me—said
Yes! And so I failed, okay, I see that, I messed up, again,
thank you, yes, I'm still that freaky little kid to be laughed
at, but I will be damned if I am crawling back out that
stupid window and not walking out the front door like
a grown man!

Dramatic
Dennis, forty-nine

Dennis is sitting on the beach on Cape Cod talking with a teenaged boy named Lucas, who has asked how he met Kitty, his wife.

DENNIS: How did we meet. Okay. The end of senior year. One of my friends, one of my wealthier friends has this party. His father invented something or discovered something. I don't know. But they have money. Mountains of money. And they have this big house in Connecticut. An estate, really. And he had this party. Beginning of summer. And I was nervous. I didn't think I'd dressed right. I had on this navy jacket and they were in tee shirts and ratty jeans. Rich people wear the filthiest clothes. So I felt awkward and I didn't talk to anyone and no one seemed interested in talking to me. The party was mostly in the living room. Or I guess it's the great room when it's that big. I wandered away. Walked out onto the patio. The sun was starting to set and the sky was this amazing shade of some color I can't name. And the land was beautiful, fields and fields of wild grass, and purple flowers. And I don't know where she came from, I mean I didn't see her before, but I looked out, into the field, and there was a girl. She was walking through the grass, with another girl. They were talking, chatting. . . And it was Kitty. And she was wearing an orange dress. And there was just enough breeze, and just enough light, and maybe just enough liquor, that I was sure, the minute I saw her, that this girl, in the orange dress in the green field, with purple flowers, was perfect. And maybe the most beautiful thing that I had ever seen. I was looking at a painting. It wasn't love. I don't mean that. It wasn't love at first sight or anything. Just a beautiful painting. A mirage. And then we talked. We got to know each other. And she seemed so. . . . scared. And that's how we met.

Information on this playwright may be found at:
www.smithandkraus.com.
Click on the WRITERS tab.

Dramatic
Will, forties

Will's estranged father, John, a former diplomat and an unabashed liberal, has asked Will to visit him at his house in upstate New York. Will, the junior senator from Tennessee and a right-wing Republican (is there any other kind?), is about to be named the running mate of his party's candidate for the presidency. John wants him to decline, and leave politics entirely, telling him that if he doesn't he will reveal to the press some deep dark secret about him.

WILL: Are you having a stroke? I'm the junior Senator from Tennessee. I sit in the same seat Ben Branch held for twenty-seven years. In three days, Drew Hanlon's going to name me his running mate. In nine weeks, I'll be Vice President-elect. I'm rather deeply involved in politics. Is this why you begged me to come up here right before the convention? You have any idea how tough it was to shake the press even to come up here?! They've been on my ass for weeks. Staff's back the hotel right now, lying their heads off to 'em. Gwynn and I had to drive up by *ourselves*. Two and a half hours in a rental with her, in the mood she's in? Thank you very much. And when I finally get here, all I find out is you've lost your mind. I could accept that you were hardly ever home as a father. You believed in what you were doing, running that puppet show in Geneva—even though *nothing*, absolutely nothing, was being decided there. And I didn't mind you claiming your deeply flawed liberal viewpoint was not political at all, but somehow above all that and wholly concerned with the welfare of mankind. I didn't even mind when you refused to admit that Reagan had you going around a Swiss mulberry bush for years while he was back here winning the Cold War. But what I do mind is you having the effrontery to think you have the right to *comment* on my political career, let alone call for an end to it. You and I have gone in very different directions, John—and we have done so because one of us is intelligent. I would suggest that you respect that intelligence and never speak to me again.

Dramatic
Eddie, thirty-one

Eddie is talking to his sister, Bridget. Their grandmother, who raised them both, has just passed away and Eddie has come home for the funeral. Here, he tells her of his earliest memory of when they moved in with Gramma.

EDDIE: Bridget . . . do you remember when we moved here? We came here in the middle of the night, and you and I were sharing the back room? The first night we were here . . . you went to sleep right away but I just . . . couldn't. After a while, I heard voices. They were getting louder and louder, but you didn't wake up. *(Pause)* I didn't know what I was supposed to do. When we went to bed, Mom told me not to leave you, no matter what happened. But the voices were scaring me. And finally I . . . I left you. As I was walking down the hall, I heard a . . . sort of thudding, clanking sound. And when I got to the bottom of the steps, Mom was lying there, and her head was bleeding. (Pause) Gramma was standing over her, and she had the big black frying pan in her hands, but she didn't seem worried that Mom was hurt, she was just . . . staring at me. We didn't say anything for a long, long time. And then I just went upstairs. I got into bed but I still couldn't sleep so I just laid awake all night. And towards dawn, I couldn't take it anymore. By then the house was totally quiet. I went down the hall, down the stairs, out to the porch. And Mom was up. Sort of. She was lying on the lounge chair. It was too cold to be sleeping there and she was just wearing shorts. When I talked to her, she didn't recognize me. I got a blanket and covered her up, but she just pushed it off and stared at it. And I went into the kitchen and Gramma had all of these vegetables in front of her, and she was chopping away and putting everything into that big, black skillet. And I said, Gramma, I think something's the matter with Mom. And Gramma just shook her head, and kept chopping, and said, "Don't worry, her whole life, she gets a little worked up. It will pass. It always does." You were upstairs but Mom just looked so . . . wrong. So I went to the porch and sat next to her. After a while I heard you come downstairs, and Gramma swept you up into this great big breakfast with all the food you liked, and you were just laughing and happy as could be. But I could hear Mom muttering something, and I went out to see what she was saying, and she just kept repeating, "Where's my baby girl?" So I went back inside, and I said, "Bridget, I think Mom wants you. She's out on the porch." And you jumped up, and you ran out there, and I could hear you laughing and squealing and Gramma just . . . if looks could kill, that would have been the end of me.

Dramatic
Tommy, sixteen

Tommy is talking to his younger sister. He got fired from his job at the Gap for smoking weed. His dad, unemployed for a year, went in to talk to the manager, an old friend, who offered him a job. Amanda is Tommy's ex-girlfriend.

TOMMY: He took my job Gabs. I mean—I know I got fired, but . . . yeah I got fired. A week ago. I've been pretending to go in . . . I just didn't want dad to feel bad . . . you know—'cause he was so proud I got the first job I applied for and everything . . . I didn't even tell him when I got promoted cause I didn't want him to feel bad about that—either . . . me moving up so quick, with him still all . . . You know . . . and it wasn't hard. The getting promoted . . . The other guys there are idiots. Including the FUCKING STORE MANAGER BILL BOWERS . . . But then Dad goes and does this . . . I mean . . . It's NOT RIGHT. He's my dad. He's not supposed to do that. Stuff like that. I mean, it's embarrassing. . . I caught Mr. Bowers . . . doing things. To Amanda. In the stockroom. He didn't know I was there. Things he shouldn't have! It was—disgusting . . . She said she had to do it or she'd lose her job and she's the one buying groceries . . . Did you know she's got four little sisters. Four . . . And then she made me swear not to tell or she'd break up with me. So I swore. And then she broke up with me anyways. So if I turn him in or whatever she'll hate me—forever—and her family will like starve! Its sooo messed up. She thinks she needs to but . . . But she's not like that. I mean—that's not who Mandy is. She's not that kind of girl. I gotta do something. I gotta think . . . I gotta figure this out . . . Things are just so fucked up. . . with like money—and jobs . . . and just . . . It's like—you gotta do what you gotta do—even if it's like—not who you really are, you know? Dad wouldn't have done this before, he's just—like—all different now—and home—and kinda just . . . you know? Mom's the only one doing okay. I mean, she's doing everything. Which is like really good, 'cause otherwise . . . We'd be like, living in a homeless shelter or something.

Seriocomic
Alvaro, early thirties

Alvaro, a playwright of Latino descent, challenges his collaborators on their decision to create a play about Danny Santiago, a reclusive young Chicano novelist. Learning that Danny is not in fact Chicano, but the literary creation of a 70 year old wealthy Anglo, Alvaro goes ballistic, and catalogues the reasons why this is a terrible idea.

ALVARO: *New York Times* crowns the kid, calls him a "new," "distinct," "streetwise," "authentic" voice from "el barrio," captures the people, rituals, language, violence, the passion, "urban grit," I'm like "Yeah, I can dig that." But when I look at the critic's name? I'm like, Huh. How much time has he spent in East LA? That a frequent stop for him? Yeah, America anything's possible, right? Maybe he's hooked in minored in Chicano Studies or is a secret card carrying member of *La Raza* got some lost branch a the family wrinkled little *abuelita* boils him up magical realist tamales that cast spells on you so butterflies fly out your asshole when you're making love? Just like in Azteca times. So yeah, maybe critics got something to back up his assertion that the goods are "authentic." The other critics all say the same thing—"authenticity this," "gritty realism that." There really that many secret Chicanos infiltrating the maitnstream press? So why *do we* take their word for it? Authentic? Fuck do they know? Worst shit? People eat that shit up! Critic says the book's "authentic"... Why? 'Cause the shit affirms every worn out cliché He picked up reading comic books. But *New York Times* says "Bitch roll over, play dead." All you bitches roll over and play dead. Everyone—critic? Public? Keep on wearing the saaaame old straitjacket.

Information on this playwright may be found at www.smithandkraus.com.
Click on the WRITERS tab.

BAUER © 2014 by Eric Coble. Reprinted by permission of Kate Navin, The Gersh Agency. For performance rights, contact Kate Navin (knavin@gershny.com).

BIG BOSSMAN © 2014 by James McManus. Reprinted by permission of Susan Gurman, Susan Gurman Agency. For performance rights, Broadway Play Publishing, (212-772-8334), (www.broadwayplaypubl.com).

BY THE WATER © 2014 by Sharyn Rothstein. Reprinted by permission of Jared Weber, ICM Partners. For performance rights, contact Dramatists Play Service, 440 Park Ave. S., New York, NY 10016 (www.dramatists.com) (212-683-8960).

CARNAVAL © 2014 by Nikkole Salter. Reprinted by permission of Nikkole Salter. For performance rights, contact Alexis Williams, Bret Adams Ltd. (awilliams@bretadamsltd.net).

CHALK FARM © 2013 by Kieran Hurley & AJ Taudevin. Reprinted by permission of Andrew Walby, Oberon Books Ltd. For performance rights, contact Susan Blakely, The Agency (sblakely@theagency.co.uk).

CHERRY SMOKE © 2006 by James McManus. Reprinted by permission of Susan Gurman, Susan Gurman Agency. For performance rights, contact Samuel French, Inc., (212-206-8990),(www.samuelfrench.com).

COLLISION © 2014 by Lyle Kessler. Reprinted by permission of Jack Tantleff, Paradigm Agency. For performance rights, contact Dramatists Play Service, 440 Park Ave. S., New York, NY 10016 (www.dramatists.com) (212-683-8960).

THE COUNTRY HOUSE © 2014 by Donald Margulies. Reprinted by permission of Zach Chotzen-Freund, Theatre Communications Group. For performance rights, contact Dramatists Play Service, 440 Park Ave. S., New York, NY 10016 (www.dramatists.com) (212-683-8960).

CONSTANT STATE OF PANIC © 2008 by Patrick Gabridge. Reprinted by permission of Patrick Gabridge. For performance rights, contact Patrick Gabridge (pat@gabridge.com).

CRACKLERS © 2014 by Cassie M. Seinuk. Reprinted by permission of Cassie M. Seinuk. For performance rights, contact Cassie M. Seinuk (cmseinuk@gmail.com).

DEAD SPECIAL CRABS © 2014 by Dan Kitrosser. Reprinted by permission of Dan Kitrosser. For performance rights, contact Jonathan Mills, Paradigm Agency (jmills@paradigmagency.com).

ENTER AT FOREST LAWN © 2014 by Mark Roberts. Reprinted by permission of Antje Oegel, AO International. For performance rights, contact Antje Oegel (aoegel@aoegelinternational.com).

THE EXCEPTIONALS © 2014 by Bob Clyman. Reprinted by permission of Alexis Willliams, Bret Adams Ltd.. For performance rights, contact Broadway Play Publishing, (212-772-8334), (www.broadwayplaypubl.com).

FAST COMPANY © 2014 by Carla Ching. Reprinted by permission of Jared Weber, ICM Partners. For performance rights, contact Val Day, ICM Partners (vday@icmpartners.com).

THE FEW © 2014 by Samuel D. Hunter. Reprinted by permission of Derek Zasky, William Morris Endeavor. For performance rights, contact Samuel French, Inc., (212-206-8990), (www.samuelfrench.com).

FREEDOM HIGH © 2014 by Adam Kraar. Reprinted by permission of Adam Kraar. For performance rights, contact Elaine Devlin (edevlinlit@aol.com).

FRIENDS AND OTHER LOVERS © 2014 by Merridith Allen. Reprinted by permission of Merridith Allen. For performance rights, contact Merridith Allen (merridith.allen26@gmail.com).

THE GROUNDLING © 2015 by Marc Palmieri. Reprinted by permission of Mary Harden, Harden-Curtis Assoc. For performance rights, contact Mary Harden (maryharden@hardencurtis.com).

HOLY LAND © 2014 by Mohamed Kacimi, transl. by Chantal Bilodeau. Reprinted by permission of Beth Blickers, Abrams Artists. For performance rights, contact Beth Blickers (beth. blickers@abramsartny.com).

THE HUNCHBACK OF SEVILLE © 2014 by Charise Castro Smith. Reprinted by permission of Jared Weber, ICM Partners. For performance rights, contact Di Glazer, ICM Partners (dglazer@icmpartners.com).

I'M GONNA PRAY FOR YOU SO HARD © 2014 by Charise Castro Smith. Reprinted by permission of Jared Weber, ICM Partners. For performance rights, Dramatists Play Service, 440 Park Ave. S., New York, NY 10016 (www.dramatists. com) (212-683-8960).

IMPENETRABLE © 2014 by Mia McCullough. Reprinted by permission of Mia McCullough. For performance rights, contact Mia McCullough (brazenhussy@miamccullough.net).

LASSO OF TRUTH © 2014 by Carson Kreitzer. Reprinted by permission of Bruce Ostler, Bret Adams Ltd. For performance rights, contact Bruce Ostler (bostler@bretadamsltd.net).

LOST LAKE © 2014 by David Auburn. Reprinted by permission of Jonathan Mills, Paradigm Agency. For performance rights, contact Dramatists Play Service, 440 Park Ave. S., New York, NY 10016 (www.dramatists.com) (212-683-8960).

THE MONEY SHOT © 2014 by Neil LaBute. Reprinted by permission of Tracy Carns, Overtook Press. For performance rights, contact Dramatists Play Service, 440 Park Ave. S., New York, NY 10016 (www.dramatists.com) (212-683-8960).

MOTHERS AND SONS © 2014 by Terrence McNally. Reprinted by permission of Amy Hasselbeck, William Morris Endeavor. For performance rights, contact Dramatists Play Service, 440 Park Ave. S., New York, NY 10016 (www.dramatists.com) (212-683-8960).

THE MUSCLES IN OUR TOES © 2014 by Stephen Belber. Reprinted by permission of Jared Weber, ICM Partners. For performance rights, contact Dramatists Play Service, 440 Park Ave. S., New York, NY 10016 (www.dramatists.com) (212-683-8960).

NDEBELE FUNERAL © 2010 by Zoey Martinson. Reprinted by permission of Zoey Martinson. For performance rights, contact Zoey Martinson (smokemirrors.co@gmail.com)

NIGHTS AT THE STRAY DOG CAFÉ © 2014 by Don Nigro. Reprinted by permission of Don Nigro. For performance rights, contact Samuel French, Inc., (212-206-8990), (www.samuelfrench.com).

POZ (+) © 2014 by Michael Aman. Reprinted by permission of Barbara Hogenson. For performance rights, contact Barbara Hogenson (bhogenson@aol.com).

THE PURPLE LIGHTS OF JOPPA ILLINOIS, © 2014 by Adam Rapp. Reprinted by permission of Rachel Viola, United Talent Agency. For performance rights, contact Rachel Viola (violar@unitedtalent.com).

REBORNING © 2015 by Zayd Dohrn. Reprinted by permission of Kate Navin, The Gersh Agency. For performance rights, contact Kate Navin (knavin@gershny.com).

REPAIRING A NATION © 2015 by Nikkole Salter. Reprinted by permission of Alexis Willliams, Bret Adams Ltd. For performance rights, contact Alexis Willliams (awilliams@bretadamsltd.net).

THE ROAD TO DAMASCUS © 2007 by Tom Dulack. Reprinted by permission of Penny Luedtke, The Luedtke Agency. For performance rights, contact Penny Luedtke (pennyagent@gmail.com).

SEX WITH STRANGERS © 2014 by Laura Eason. Reprinted by permission of Tracy Carns, Overtook Press. For performance rights, contact Dramatists Play Service, 440 Park Ave. S., New York, NY 10016 (www.dramatists.com) (212-683-8960).

SMALL WORLD © 2012 by Frederick Stroppel. Reprinted by permission of Frederick Stroppel. For performance rights, contact Frederick Stroppel (fredstrop@aol.com).

SMOKE © 2014 by Kim Davies. Reprinted by permission of Jared Weber, ICM Partners. For performance rights, contact Di Glazer, ICM Partners (dglazer@icmpartners.com).

SPACEBAR: A BROADWAY PLAY BY KYLE SUGARMAN © 2011 by Michael Mitnick. Reprinted by permission of Amy Hasselbeck, William Morris Endeavor. For performance rights, contact Playscripts, Inc.(www.playscripts. com).

STALKING THE BOGEYMAN © 2014 by Markus Potter. Reprinted by permission of Joseph Rosswog, Daryl Roth Theatrical Licensing. For performance rights, contact Joseph Rosswog (josephr@darylrothlicensing.com)

TAKE ME BACK © 2013 by Emily Schwend. Reprinted by permission of Beth Blickers, Abrams Artists. For performance rights, contact Beth Blickers (beth.blickers@abramsartny.com).

TEATIME AT GOLGOTHA © 2014 by Mark Chrisler. Reprinted by permission of Mark Chrisler. For performance rights, contact Broadway Play Publishing, (212-772-8334), (www.broadwayplaypubl.com).

TOO MUCH SUN © 2014 by Nicky Silver. Reprinted by permission of Amy Hasselbeck, William Morris Endeavor. For performance rights, contact Dramatists Play Service, 440 Park Ave. S., New York, NY 10016 (www.dramatists.com) (212-683-8960).

THE VELOCITY OF AUTUMN © 2014 by Eric Coble. Reprinted by permission of Kate Navin, The Gersh Agency. For performance rights, contact Dramatists Play Service, 440 Park Ave. S., New York, NY 10016 (www.dramatists. com) (212-683-8960).

A VIEW OF THE MOUNTAINS © 2014 by Lee Blessing. Reprinted by permission of Lee Blessing. For performance rights, contact Dramatists Play Service, 440 Park Ave. S., New York, NY 10016 (www.dramatists.com) (212-683-8960).